the
Child-Friendly
Food Allergy
Cookbook

the Child-Friendly Food Allergy Cookbook

MORE THAN 150 RECIPES THAT ARE:

* Wheat-Free
* Gluten-Free
* Dairy-Free
* Nut-Free
* Egg-Free
* Low in Sugar

LESLIE HAMMOND AND LYNNE MARIE ROMINGER

FOREWORD BY KEVIN A. TRACY, M.D.,
SPECIALIST IN PEDIATRIC INTERNAL MEDICINE
AT THE UC DAVIS MEDICAL GROUP

APPLE

Text © 2004 by Leslie Hammond and Lynne Marie Rominger

Published in the UK in 2004 by
Apple Press
Sheridan House
112-116A Western Road
Hove
East Sussex BN3 1DD
England

10 9 8 7 6 5 4 3 2

ISBN 1-84092-449-7

Book design: *tabula rasa* graphic design
Cover design: Mary Ann Smith
Illustrations © 2004 www.clipart.com

Printed and bound in Canada

The information in this book is for educational purposes only. It is not intended to replace the advice of a physician or medical practitioner. Please see your health care provider before beginning any new health program.

CONTENTS

Foreword	9
Introduction	11
Shopping for Food	13
Snacks	19
Meals	89
Side Dishes	141
Sweets and Treats	153
Helpful Hints	217
Index	220

ACKNOWLEDGMENTS

Thank you to my sweet little girls Wendy, Allison, and Madeline! Thank you to my husband, my mom and dad, my teenage brothers and their voracious appetites, and to my giant loving family (too many to name!). I'd like to make a special thanks to all the incredible women in my life who have believed in me and helped me through this book—Beth S., Kimberly M., Lynne, Jennifer S., and Jenny C., I couldn't have done this without you! Thank you to my girls' teacher Mrs. Sims and their fabulous school. I would also like to thank KXTV-News 10, KCRA-TV 3, and KMAX-TV 31, in Sacramento, California, for bringing me on their respective shows and helping show families how to cook delicious foods allergy-free. Thank you to Mike Dunne of the *Sacramento Bee, Sacramento* magazine, and the Davis Enterprise for writing stories about my cooking mission. And thank you to Dr. Kevin Tracey for helping me when I was little and again for your wise Foreword. Finally, thank you to everyone at Fair Winds who helped me make this book a reality.

—*Leslie Hammond*

Thank you Jennifer Basye Sander for bringing me in contact with Leslie and for being my friend and mentor. You are an amazingly talented, witty, and selfless woman who brings wisdom to my world. Thank you Leslie Hammond for your incredible recipes and passion for helping children; I've thoroughly enjoyed working with you and sharing everything from schooling ideas to home remedies to girl talk. Thank you to my parents and children; you are always so patient with all my work. Thank you "Dreamy" for providing some sweet respite for "Toula" amidst all my writing deadlines. You challenge me intellectually and make my knees weak. I feel blessed to have you as my friend. Thanks to the always-inspiring Derek Fromages; daily you brought levity to my life, and I doubt I could make it without the laughter you ignite. Thank you Christy Flis for your research, writing, and work on this book—what an amazing personal assistant you've been. A million "thank-yous" to Sabina Duncan. When I am frazzled and over-whelmed, you take the helm and lead me home. Thank you to everyone at Fair Winds—especially Paula Munier. I think you and I are kindred spirits, Paula; I look forward to working with you on many more projects. Finally, thank you, my Lord and Savior, Jesus Christ. I can do nothing without You.

—*Lynne Marie Rominger*

FOREWORD

"What's for dinner?" "Is there anything to eat?" "Can I have some of that?" Not a day goes by that thoughts of food do not enter our minds, pushing aside whatever else is in there when we are hungry. Moreover, we eat if we are happy; we eat if we are sad. We celebrate big events and those smaller special moments with food. We socialize over brunch, meet family for lunch, and get together with old friends for dinner. In times of trouble, eating comforts us. And what would holidays and birthdays, weddings and graduations be like without their associated feasts, potlucks, and special dishes? Take away the social nature of our food and there most certainly would be a revolution. Like water and shelter, we need food to live. Food is a need of humans on many levels. Of course physiological, but also emotional!

So what happens when food—that which we desire, crave, and need—makes us ill? We may stay too long at the feasting table and then suffer later; we may even eat something that has questionable origins but an exotic aroma or appearance that makes the risk of illness worth taking. For many people, however, food can cause more problems than temporary indigestion or gastrointestinal furor. Food intolerances and allergies can cause everything from chronic aches and pains to life-threatening reactions. Identifying and avoiding offending foods may be simple or it may drastically alter your life. When, for example, milk is the problem, suddenly it becomes amazing how many recipes and favorite dishes contain dairy products. It's not easy for adults to stay clear of whatever foods may harm them; it's even more difficult for children.

What does a child with a food allergy do at a birthday party, school, or at a friend's house when something wonderful is served that contains something "bad"? Saying, "No, thank you" when everyone else is gobbling up the delicious treat is hard to do. Should you just try a little, so no one will think you are contrary or weird, risking turning red with hives and stopping breathing or suffering with stomachaches for days? Such are the dilemmas faced by those trying to eat the right thing.

As a pediatrician, I see many parents who believe their child's various complaints and problems are due to food allergies. Most are not, and when there are specific food interactions, they are usually not true allergies but are common reactions and intolerances. Even so, some parents become afraid to feed their infants or children for fear of what may happen. But then there are those children who suffer with true food allergies, which make their eczema and asthma worse, may cause poor growth, can cause horrible intestinal problems, or can suddenly bring about severe breathing trouble. Daily life can prove simple or hard—depending upon how easy it is to eliminate and avoid the offending food, and how cooperative the child is at following the food rules. Unfortunately, that which is forbidden quickly becomes more attractive. Moreover, others unaware the offered food is a no-no, and potentially life-threatening for the child, may give gifts, treats, and free samples.

One food that causes allergic reactions, wheat, is often called the "staff of life." But wheat can be the "disrupter of sleep" and "spoiler of play" for those with wheat and gluten sensitivities and allergies—as it was for an author of this book, Leslie Hammond.

I met Leslie when she was a child, trying to figure out why she had such bad belly pains and so many gastrointestinal problems. No one could figure out what was wrong with Leslie. After a hospitalization, I tested Leslie for many possibilities before we figured out what was ailing her, why Leslie suffered so much. Food—"the staff of life," in particular—was making Leslie sick. The cookies that she craved and the toast that she was eating because it was "bland" and she figured everything else would further upset her stomach were actually the culprits. But what foods that kids eat don't have wheat? What could Leslie eat? Well, from the motivation of personal experience, she has been successful in finding ways to enjoy mealtime without suffering later. This cookbook is to help families faced with the challenge of feeding the kids when foods are forbidden.

Leslie proves food can still be fun and the centerpiece of life's parties—even when food limitations are an issue. She manages this feat by putting the "usual" ingredients back on the shelf and replacing them with others you may have never used or never thought you could use. Recipes may at first taste or look a tad different, but with a happy body comes a happy mind, and soon we have new foods to comfort the soul and to answer the eternal question, "Isn't there anything else to eat?" Feeding a child with food allergies can be challenging for parents. All kids want yummy "kid standard" fare like macaroni and cheese and spaghetti. All kids want a chocolate chip cookie now and then! With this book, every child gets a cookie, thanks to Leslie.

Kevin A. Tracy, MD
Pediatric Internal Medicine
UC Davis Medical Group
Sacramento, California

INTRODUCTION

In a world full of sweets, treats, and fun foods like pizza, it's extremely difficult to be the child who is allergic to everything everyone else eats. So many of the menu items include wheat and dairy as staple ingredients—precisely the items that cause the most trouble for children and adults who suffer from food allergies. Think about what the favorite foods of most kids are. Perhaps, pizza, spaghetti, chicken nuggets, and macaroni and cheese top the list. Now think about what their favorite sweets and treats are. Ask them and most will include cookies, cupcakes, and brownies high on the list. And all those delights just mentioned—from the nuggets to the cupcakes—contain wheat flour and/or dairy elements. So what can a mom feed a hungry child who can't eat anything?

I have the answer because I was one of those children with food allergies. Until finally diagnosed with multiple food allergies, I endured a childhood beset by illness after illness. By my preteens, after a lengthy hospitalization, one doctor finally figured out why I was so sick all the time. But a diagnosis didn't end the heartache. In fact, my suffering was only beginning. I went home from the hospital to watch my siblings and parents eat everything delicious and appealing to the palate that I couldn't. On my thirteenth birthday, my friends and family sat down to a Baskin Robbins ice cream cake while I was handed a rice cracker! No wonder I hid bags of chocolate chip cookies in my closet and ate clandestinely, only to get sick again and again. The hard part I had to live with was being a normal person who felt abnormal because I had nothing to eat. If I ate what my friends and family ate, I would become sick. But even though I felt abnormal, I really wasn't that different, because so many people suffer with food allergies. According to the National Institute of Allergy and Infectious Diseases, "food allergy occurs in 8 percent of children and in 1–2 percent of adults. Approximately 100 Americans, usually children, die annually from food-induced anaphylaxis." Currently, 5–8 million Americans are allergic to a food. Strict avoidance of the restricted food is the only way to avoid a reaction, extreme illness, and, in some cases, even death.

Recognizing the importance of avoiding wheat in my diet, I was determined to find a way to eat and enjoy delicious meals that wouldn't make me sick. So I started finding healthy substitutes and creating yummy foods that I could eat. When I started having children of my own (surprise: all with food allergies), I committed myself to finding ways to include the whole family in tasty repast and treats without any wheat and/or dairy. *The Kid-Friendly Food Allergy Cookbook* is built from my experience and includes realistic recipes for moms and dads of food-allergic families. All of my recipes are the types of dishes that you see kids eating at school, parties, and on the covers of magazines. Helpful suggestions for substitutions—to help you with all allergy needs—are included with many of the recipes. For example, PB and Banana Chip Muffin (page 80) may be made dairy-free, nut-free, egg-free, and also low in sugar, depending on the affliction of the child.

The primary focus of the recipes in this book is gluten-free. If you do not have problems with gluten, you can easily replace the flours in these recipes with your preferred flour. Where once I was banned from eating pizza and cake on my birthday, I proudly show you parents how to make a potato-crusted pizza worthy of a trendy bistro and an orange-vanilla cake one might find in a "make-your-mouth-water" pastry shop. I've managed to offer bakery-style muffins instead of bland and funny-tasting foods to hungry allergy-suffering mouths. My commitment to you and your family is clear: Every child deserves a cookie.

A goal of my cookbook is that you can walk into your local supermarket and purchase any and all ingredients you need to cook for your family—that you needn't travel to some health food store or specialty market to make dinner. Please refer to the shopping section of this cookbook for guidance.

Because I was hungry, I succeeded in making great-tasting common foods like pancakes and Hot and Yummy Pockets like the store brand, all allergy-free. Because I feel so adamantly that every child deserves to feel included at mealtime, I've gathered my recipes for your family in this cookbook. You can buy or make foods for the whole family that taste wonderful. Your child will love being part of the function of eating and not the "poor kid" who can't eat anything.

IN AN EGG SHELL

Eggs play an important role in both the texture and taste of your foods, and eliminating them from baking can be one of the biggest obstacles in the kitchen. When removed, cakes and cookies may become crumbly or flat, and replacements for the egg may vary, too. Each egg substitution in this book is given to replace the *purpose* of the egg in the baked good. Egg yolks contribute to the creamy taste in my Apple Rice Pudding, an egg acts as a binder in the Ricotta cream for the enchiladas, and the beaten egg acts as your leavener in a birthday cake. Dry egg replacement is the best substitution for most of the recipes, but not all. For example, the Creamsicle Cake gets its soft, fluffy texture by incorporating air into the egg whites. There is just no way to substitute the egg's function in this particular recipe, or recipes like this.

The egg substitution will yield different results depending on the fat/sugar ratio in your baked good. In some recipes I simply omit the egg to achieve a successful result; in others I may replace it with an additional banana. (Remember, though, that a banana may work in a recipe such as banana bread, but won't work in your enchiladas or chocolate cake!) When a food requires more binding or a firm texture, I add the dry egg replacement. You can rest assured—I have tested all of these recipes over the past ten years, and developed substitutions that give the best results according to taste and texture. There are a few recipes that do not have egg variations, but I do try to suggest an alternative recipe in its place.

SHOPPING FOR FOOD

I come across many families who believe that once their child is diagnosed with a food allergy or intolerance that they must search in expensive specialty stores and health food stores for substitute ingredients and special ingredients. Not so. In my cooking, for example, I use rice flour instead of wheat flour for all recipes. One might think that rice flour is difficult to procure and requires driving all over town to find. It isn't. I buy all my rice flour—all my ingredients, in fact—at my local grocery store. I talked with the manager of the grocery store and requested Bob's Red Mill White Rice Flour. He was able to order the flour and keep it stocked, too. Basically, there are just a couple of steps to getting any ingredient into your supermarket that you may need to feed your child. They are:

Call the store and ask if the item is stocked. If it is, go buy it. If not, ask the manager to order the item or ask for a request form and fill it out. Many stores provide request forms for just this reason—although I have found that speaking with the manager in person seems to get the product on the shelves more expediently. That's it! I've only had a problem once with a clerk who told me that something couldn't be ordered because they didn't have room on the shelves. Once I talked to the manager, however, the item could indeed be ordered and kept continuously on the shelf.

Beyond buying your ingredients at the local grocery store, another goal of mine is that you can make dinner for about the same price as you would if you could eat the toxic foods. Gluten-free items are becoming more attainable in mainstream shopping. Dairy-free milks are available everywhere. Egg-free and peanut-free items are still a bit more challenging and do require more health food stores and online purchasing. Again, always talk to your local store manager about ordering items you need. You will be happily surprised at what they are able to order!

What follows is a list of some of the best products I've found to help you on your healthy, allergy-free eating quest. I certainly haven't tested everything out there, but I've tried many things. I've decided on the following products by taste, convenience, and accessibility. If you are looking for convenience items only, your best bet is to go online to www.glutenfreemarket.com for a list of new and successful packaged foods and mixes.

On to some top choices.

BREADS

Ener-G Foods—tapioca, white rice, and brown rice breads (perfect for grilled cheese, toast, croutons, and bread crumbs) for less than $4.00 per loaf. Available in health food stores and online.

Food for Life—rice pecan and rice almond (perfect for PB&Js, cold sandwiches, French toast, and traditional toast), priced between $2.60 and $3.50 a loaf. Available in large grocery stores, health food stores, Trader Joe's, and online.

Cause You're Special—offers fairly inexpensive, easy-to-use bread mixes. Available online.

Bob's Red Mill—bread mixes and flours, priced between $2.00 and $4.00. Available in health food stores and large grocery stores.

PASTA

De Boles—spirals, penne, and noodle shapes that are great served in cold salads or with sauces, priced under $3.00. Available in most stores if requested.

Tinkyada—all noodle shapes. My favorite pasta because it's easy to make and the most wheat-like in taste and texture. Available in health food stores and some large grocery stores. Try to get a hold of their lasagna noodles; they are awesome!

Lundberg Rice—many pasta shapes. Easily found in most grocery stores and easy to order if not.

Glutano—rice pasta in fun shapes like animals; ready-to-go Macaroni and Cheese; products priced between $1.00 and $5.00. Mainly available online.

DAIRY

Lactaid—the milk is gluten-free, but the ice cream is not.

Philadelphia brand cream cheese is gluten-free.

Tillamook dairy products are gluten-free; check the ingredients list on flavored ice creams.

Kraft Cool Whip is gluten-free.

Call Kraft at 1-800-323-0768 for a long list of gluten-free foods. Jell-O products, for example, are part of Kraft Foods; many pudding flavors are gluten-free, egg-free, and yummy!

Jell-O puddings contain dairy but are egg- and gluten-free.

Pacific Rice drinks are gluten-free and dairy-free.

Imagine Foods makes great dairy-free and egg-free puddings.

WARNING: Be very careful when purchasing dairy-free cheese. Most contain casein and whey, potential irritants. Consult your doctor about trying Swiss cheese, cottage cheese, and Parmesan. Some people with dairy intolerances are able to use these products. Just check to make sure they are also gluten-free!

SNACKS

Read the ingredients of your favorite chips and snack items. Chances are, they don't have (never had) wheat in them! I recommend calling consumer information toll-free numbers to double-check. If you are leery about gluten in things like food colorings in fruit snacks, go online to a vendor you trust and order a gluten-free known brand. Pay careful attention to all fried foods for peanut and tree nut ingredients if your child suffers from a nut allergy.

Call your local major grocery store's customer service number and ask them for a list of their brand's allergy-free info. Safeway in Northern California sent me an impressive list from soups to puddings.

Need a good peanut-free book? I suggest the *Peanut Allergy Answer Book* by Michael Young.

Vans—gluten-free waffle varieties priced well and available almost anywhere. Dairy-free, egg-free, and gluten-free, who needs to make them when they are so easy to buy!

Over the Internet or in some large grocery stores, you can even find gluten-free ice cream cones.

Lundberg Farms—rice cakes, priced at around $2.00–$3.00; these rice cakes are not only tasty, but they hold up well for things like pizza snacks and jelly.

Real Foods—multigrain corn thins; we eat these with cream cheese on top just like a bagel. Priced under $3.00 at most grocery stores.

Barbara's—some of the cereals are gluten-free.

Uncle Ben's Cream of Rice cereal—available everywhere. I insist you try their Lemon Blueberry muffin recipe on the back of their box—just replace the regular flour with rice flour.

EnviroKids—tasty cereals with many varieties that make great snacks for kids.

· ·

Remember the snacks that never had gluten or allergens—fruits and vegetables!

· ·

SWEETS

Pamela's—the cookies are available almost everywhere, are reasonably priced, and are great as a quick treat on the go.

Vermont Nut Free Chocolates—particularly wonderful for children who have nut allergies. Parents won't need to worry about cross-contamination with these chocolates. Available online or through your health food store.

Ener-G—great selection of prepackaged chocolate cakes, cookies, and brownies. Available online at www. ener-g.com.

There is a lot out there for gluten-free. Be very careful to check ingredients when a peanut or egg allergy exists.

FLOURS AND BAKING NEEDS

My favorite pick is *Bob's Red Mill* white and brown rice flours. The items are reasonably priced between $2.00 and $4.00, and this flour provides the best texture. You can find it in most stores, but if not, it should be easy to order in your store.

You can also buy flour in bulk online from *Ener-G Foods* (www.ener-g.com).

Baking powders and baking sodas sometimes include dairy elements and aluminum. Look in your health food store or go online to order dairy-free, aluminum-free alternatives.

I prefer to use *Cook's* powdered vanilla. *Imitation Vanilla* is great and inexpensive.

Spectrums nonhydrogenated shortening, margarine, and oils allow you to have holding texture—like in my Fun Cut-Outs (page 166), without any nasty hydrogenated oil or dairy.

I recommend using sugars that are naturally from cane sugar; generic sugar is often beet sugar with dyes. If you have a child with diabetes or are looking for sugarless items, I highly recommend a substitute sugar called *Whey Low,* currently only available online at www.wheylow.com. Read their allergy info—for it does have corn and dairy elements. I do not recommend any artificial sweetners.

Check the ice cream sprinkles at your grocery stores; they are mainly gluten-free. Perfect to decorate any cookie or cake.

Nestlé's Tollhouse Chocolate Chips are gluten-free and dairy-free.

Ener-G Chocolate Chips are gluten-free and dairy-free.

Many people have contacted me regarding the gluten in corn syrup. *Kraft's* corn syrup is gluten-free.

Look in your health food store for gluten-free *Tamari* soy sauce, or order online.

As egg replacements go, my favorite is the powdered *Ener-G Egg Replacer.* You can purchase it for about $5.69 in health food stores or online. You can use this replacement for other recipes that call for xanthum gum. I use this to add texture in shortbreads and for my egg-free cooking.

SEASONINGS/SYRUPS

Knorr chicken and beef bouillon are gluten-free.

Log Cabin and *Mrs. Butterworth's* are gluten-free.

Cornstarch, potato starch, rice starch, and tapioca starch can all be substituted for each other.

A NOTE REGARDING MEASUREMENTS

Unless otherwise stated, for all liquid measurements, 1 cup = 225 milliliters. For all solid measurements, metric conversions are provided.

SNACKS

Healthy snacks are part of a healthy diet. Children, in particular, need several snacks per day for good nutrition and energy. In this section, you'll find ideas to feed your little ones in-between meals.

APPLESAUCES

My children and I enjoy applesauce in many different ways. We like to use it as a dip, to smother pancakes with, and added in baked goods. You can omit the sugar in all variations and still get a pleasantly sweet snack. For an interesting variation, try using pears.

Basic Applesauce
Serves 8

1½ pounds (680 grams) apples, cored, peeled, and cut into 1-inch chunks

½ cup water*

1 tablespoon lemon juice

1. In a medium saucepan, add apples, water, and lemon juice.
2. Cook covered on medium heat for 10 to 15 minutes until apples are soft and water is evaporated.
3. Take pan off burner and let cool.
4. When cool, blend in a food processor or blender until it reaches the consistency you prefer.
5. Cool completely and store in sealed plastic container for up to one week.

* Unless otherwise stated, for all liquid measurements, 1 cup = 225 milliliters.

THIS JUST IN: Apple Eating Great for Your Heart! Researchers at the University of California Davis Medical School studied how eating apples and drinking apple juice every day affects heart disease risk. Participants did not change their diets at all with the exception of including apples every day for twelve weeks; in the end, they had reduced their risk of heart disease. Apples contain a variety of antioxidant phytochemicals that decrease LDL oxidation. Oxidized LDL cholesterol is more likely to build up in arteries, a process that can cause heart attacks and stroke. So start your child now on a habit of eating apples to ensure a long, healthy life.

WANT TO KNOW a great fruit to add to your child's diet if he or she is getting leg cramps or has sore muscles from athletics? The answer is: an apple. One medium apple offers the eater 159 milligrams of potassium. Good-bye sore muscles!

YOU'VE PROBABLY HEARD that an apple a day keeps the doctor away, right? Well, guess what? An apple a day may just help your child maintain a healthy heart for life because the fruit is a great source of soluble fiber. Soluble fiber like pectin actually helps to prevent cholesterol buildup in the lining of blood vessel walls, thus reducing the incidence of arteriosclerosis and heart disease. So go ahead and eat that apple every day!

Blue Applesauce
Serves 8

Basic Applesauce recipe
⅔ cup (100 grams) frozen blueberries
¼ cup (50 grams) sugar (optional)

1. Prepare Basic Applesauce recipe per directions, but add berries and sugar with apples.

Pink Applesauce
Serves 8

Basic Applesauce recipe
⅔ cup (100 grams) frozen strawberries or raspberries
½ cup (100 grams) sugar (optional)

1. Prepare Basic Applesauce recipe, adding berries and sugar at the same time as the apples.

Cinnamon Applesauce
Serves 8

Basic Applesauce recipe
2 teaspoons cinnamon
¼ cup (50 grams) sugar
Pinch of salt

1. Prepare Basic Applesauce recipe, adding cinnamon, sugar, and salt with apples.

Low-Sugar Variation: Use Whey Low.

Applesauce Parfait
Serves 2

This recipe makes plenty for two large, healthy, and yummy snacks. Use your imagination with different fruits.

2 cups (500 grams) applesauce, homemade
   or store bought
½ cup (80 grams) frozen or fresh blueberries,
   strawberries, or peaches
½ cup (60 grams) crunchy granola

1. Fill two parfait cups with ¼ cup (60 grams) of applesauce each. Layer fruit next, then granola.
2. Repeat the layering, ending with a sprinkle of granola on the top of the parfait.

AND YET ANOTHER REASON to keep feeding your wee ones those ripe red apples! Researchers in the United Kingdom recently reported that people who eat five or more apples a week have better lung function and lower risk of asthma and other respiratory disease compared to people who rarely eat apples. The ten-year study out of the University of Nottingham of 2,633 people examined the relationship between diet and respiratory health. The researchers suspect that antioxidants in apples lead to these health benefits.

AS A PARENT, you know that your children should eat a colorful plate of fruits and vegetables to ensure they receive all the nutrients they need to grow up healthy. But do you know what it is in fruits and veggies that researchers are learning really helps our health? They're phytochemicals! Over 4,000 phytochemicals have been identified and are produced by various plants to help protect them from insects, diseases, and other threats to their health. Those same substances act to protect human health, too. And all we have to do for this "health" insurance is to eat five servings a day!

Rainbow Happy Healthy Juice
Serves 5

This juice is a great way to "sneak" extra fruits and veggies into your child's diet. My children named this juice.

3 apples, cored and sectioned

2 oranges, peeled and sectioned

4 large carrots, peeled

½ cup (30 grams) chopped fresh parsley

1 pear, cored and sectioned

2 celery stalks

1. Use juicer according to manufacturer's directions.

2. Let children stir the juice and watch the rainbow of colors all combine.

Horchata Rice Drink
Serves 4

Almost like a smoothie, this unusual drink makes a fill-ing snack. This is Mexican rice water or rice milk. It is an excellent dessert as well.

1 cup (200 grams) uncooked white rice

1 cup (150 grams) toasted almonds and/or any berries

3 cups water, boiled

1 teaspoon vanilla

½ teaspoon cinnamon

Honey to taste

1. Place rice in a food processor. With the metal blade attach-ment, pulse for about 2 minutes or until rice is powdery. If using almonds, add them now and process until ground. Set aside.

2. Add three cups of boiled water to the rice mixture. Add vanilla and cinnamon to mixture. Cover and place in the refrigerator for at least 3 hours (or overnight).

3. Transfer water-rice mixture into the food processor and add desired berries. Process until smooth. Sweeten with honey to taste.

4. Serve over ice. Keep any unused portion refrigerated and drink within the day.

Low-Sugar Variation: *Sweeten with Whey Low.*

Nut-Free Variation: *Omit almonds*

MANY PEOPLE who are allergic to cow milk products or who suffer from lactose intolerance can enjoy goat yogurt. Yogurt cultures convert lactose into lactic acid, making yogurt easier to digest than milk. Lactobacillus acido-philus and bifidus can help to restore normal intestinal flora after antibiotic therapy.

Frozen Fruit and Yogurt
Serves 8

Kids won't know that they're eating a healthy snack with these frozen fruit and yogurt treats; they'll think they're getting dessert before dinner! My children especially like these after a hot day in the park.

2 cups (500 grams) plain soy, goat, or dairy yogurt

1 cup (200 grams) fruit (for example, ½ cup each bananas and strawberries, or tinned peaches and blueberries)

¼ cup (85 grams) honey, optional

1. Puree all ingredients in a blender.
2. Freeze in a casserole dish for 30 minutes.
3. Blend again and pour into Popsicle molds or back into the casserole dish. Freeze for 1 to 2 hours.
4. Use an ice cream scoop for the baking dish and scoop frozen mixture into balls.
5. Serve with fresh fruit, low-sugar cookies, or granola.

Dairy-Free Variation: Use soy or goat yogurt.

Frozen Yogurt Sandwiches
Serves 8

Use your creativity with the fillings of this snack. I like chocolate sorbet, my husband likes peach ice cream, and my kids like strawberry frozen yogurt. You can make these bars as small or as large as you want. Just keep the cookie cutting at an even number.

⅓ cup (85 grams) butter

½ cup (100 grams) brown sugar

2 tablespoons (40 grams) light corn syrup

2 cups (200 grams) oats or buckwheat flakes

½ cup (35 grams) shredded dried coconut or
   sliced almonds

1 teaspoon vanilla

¼ teaspoon salt

4 cups (700 grams) purchased or homemade
   frozen yogurt, thawed slightly

1. Line a 10-inch × 15-inch baking pan with parchment paper.
2. In a large saucepan, melt ⅓ cup butter on medium heat, stirring often.
3. Remove from heat and add sugar, corn syrup, oats, coconut, vanilla, and salt.
4. Mix until well blended.
5. Pour onto lined baking pan and press mixture down evenly with a long metal spatula.

PERHAPS YOU KNOW your child responds better to a gluten-free or wheat-free diet but no doctor has ever diagnosed your child as having celiac disease or a food allergy. Go to www.enterolab.com for more information about ordering a gluten sensitivity test that you and your children may take in the privacy of your home.

6. Bake at 375°F (190°C) for about 10 minutes or until browned and bubbling all over. Remove and let cool to room temperature.

7. With a sharp metal spatula, cut bar into 36 small matching rectangles.

8. Place 18 of the rectangle bars, smooth side down, side by side in a single layer on another lined 10-inch × 15-inch baking pan to make a firm large rectangle in half of the pan.

9. Spoon frozen yogurt over the entire cookie surface until it is evenly covered, about 2 inches all over. (If yogurt gets too slushy, refreeze for 10 minutes or so).

10. Match remaining cookies over yogurt to make a sandwich. Cover and freeze for 4 hours.

11. Remove from freezer and with a metal spatula cut out each rectangle bar, following the edges of the cookie pattern. Trim sandwich edges evenly if you like.

12. Serve or wrap in parchment and place in a freezer bag for up to two weeks.

Dairy-Free Variation: *Substitute margarine for butter and use soy frozen yogurt.*

Low-Sugar Variation: *Substitute ¼ cup Whey Low for brown sugar and 2 tablespoons of sugar-free maple syrup for corn syrup. Omit coconut.*

Nut-Free Variation: *Omit almonds.*

Fruit and Marshmallow Sauce
Serves 10

Dip your favorite fruits with this easy, kid-approved sauce that also makes a great frosting for cupcakes and muffins!

1 16-ounce (455-gram) jar of marshmallow crème

1 8-ounce (225-gram) package cream cheese

2 teaspoons fruit juice/nectar (mandarin orange, strawberry, peach, etc.)

Orange zest, if desired

1. Blend all ingredients in a food processor until smooth.
2. Spoon into a bowl and arrange fresh fruit around bowl. Apples, pineapple spears, and strawberries are our favorites.

Dairy-Free Variation: Mix with tofu cream cheese or soy yogurt.

WANT TO FIND OUT more information about celiac disease? Interested in finding a support group in your area? Navigate online to www.celiac.org, the Web site of the Celiac Disease Foundation.

Whipped Fruit Butter
Makes about 2 cups

You choose whatever flavor you prefer from different types of dried fruits in this simple recipe that's tasty on crackers and toasted allergy-free breads. It even works to frost your muffins!

1½ cups (225 grams) dried fruit pieces (apricots, apples, blueberries, etc.)

1 stick of butter, room temperature

2 tablespoons (40 grams) honey (optional)

1. Put fruit in the food processor and pulse until fruit is relatively smooth, with some chunks.

2. Add the butter and honey; process for a minute or so until you have a desired chunk consistency. You may puree until smooth like butter, too.

3. Spread on breads or crackers.

Dairy-Free Variation: *Use margarine.*

Hale and Hearty Fruit Dip
Makes about 2 cups (450 grams)

Though this dip is traditionally eaten with fruit or plain rice crackers, try using it as a filling for a crepe or topping for a pancake. It is a healthy alternative to syrup.

1 cup (245 grams) yogurt or cottage cheese

1 tablespoon (20 grams) honey (optional)

½ firm banana (optional)

⅓ cup (50 grams) fresh or frozen berries

Squeezed juice from ½ fresh orange

1. Place all ingredients in a food processor and blend until smooth.
2. Refrigerate for 30 minutes and serve with fruit or rice crackers.

Dairy-Free Variation: *Use soy or goat yogurt.*

FOR MORE HELPFUL information about managing your child's allergy to gluten, contact the Gluten Intolerance Group of North America either by calling 206-246-6652 or by logging on to www.gluten.net.

JICAMA (pronounced "hee-ca-ma") is a tropical legume that produces an edible fleshy taproot. It is native to Mexico and northern Central America and is widely cultivated there and in Southeast Asia. Jicama is most commonly eaten fresh. After the fibrous brown outer tissue of the root is peeled away, the crisp white flesh can be sliced, diced, or cut into strips for use as a garnish, in salads, or with dips. It is frequently served as a snack, sprinkled with lime or lemon juice and a dash of chili powder. Jicama remains crisp after boiling and serves as a textural substitute for water chestnuts. Jicama is similar in food value to white potatoes, but with slightly fewer calories.

Spinach Dip
Makes about 3 cups (700 grams)

Treat your children to a snack worthy of Popeye and packing a punch of vitamin A. By choosing carrots for dipping instead of crackers or bread, you'll give your little ones a beta-carotene wallop, too. What a yummy way to get in several servings of veggies a day.

1 cup (235 grams) mayonnaise

1 16-ounce (455-gram) tub sour cream

1 teaspoon tamari

¼ cup (30 grams) each fresh, finely chopped red peppers, parsley, and spring onions

½ cup (65 grams) chopped white onion

¼ cup (30 grams) finely chopped jicama (optional)

1 8-ounce (225-gram) package frozen chopped spinach, thawed and drained

1 8-ounce (225-gram) can water chestnuts, drained and chopped

1 teaspoon black pepper

¼ teaspoon cayenne pepper

1. In a large bowl mix mayonnaise, sour cream, tamari, bell pepper, parsley, onions, and jicama.
2. Stir in spinach, water chestnuts, black pepper, and cayenne pepper. Refrigerate for 30 minutes and serve.

Dairy-Free Variation: Use soy, plain-style yogurt, or sour cream substitute.

Egg-Free Variation: Use egg-free mayonnaise.

Bean Dip
Makes about 2 cups (500 grams)

My family's favorite bean to use in this dip is chickpeas (also called garbanzo beans)—making this dip much like Middle Eastern hummus. Calling this bean dip instead of hummus may make it more appealing to some three-year-olds.

1 15-ounce (420-gram) can of beans (chickpea/garbanzo, black, navy, or pinto), undrained

1 tablespoon lemon juice

2 teaspoons minced garlic

¼ teaspoon salt

½ teaspoon cayenne pepper

1 tablespoon chopped coriander

2 tablespoons olive oil or sesame oil

Veggies of your choice for dipping

Tortilla chips for dipping

1. In a food processor, blend all ingredients except veggies and tortilla chips until smooth. Add more oil if you prefer a thinner, smoother dip or drain the beans if you like a thicker paste.

2. Cover and keep refrigerated. Use within the day.

3. Cut veggies into long spears. Place a bowl of dip in the center of a plate and arrange veggies and tortilla chips around the bowl.

"WATER-SOLUBLE fiber prevalent in oat bran, oatmeal, citrus fruit, and most types of beans seems to help clean out cholesterol. Round, irregularly shaped, buff-colored legumes, chickpeas are also called garbanzo beans or ceci. When you accompany chickpeas with vitamin C rich foods like green peppers, the body makes better use of their nonheme iron." (Source: *Prevention* magazine's *Nutrition Advisor*, p. 35)

Mexican Five-Layer Dip
Serves 8

Serve this favorite with tortilla chips or heated corn tortillas. Though mainly served as a snack, we sometimes make a meal out of this hearty dip.

1 16-ounce (455-gram) can refried beans

1 cup (230 grams) sour cream

1 cup (120 grams) shredded Colby cheese

1 cup (250 grams) guacamole

1 cup (260 grams) salsa or diced fresh tomatoes

1. In an 8-inch baking dish, spread the beans on the bottom. Layer the sour cream, guacamole, salsa, and, lastly, the cheese. Serve immediately or cover and refrigerate for up to 24 hours.

Dairy-Free Variation: *Replace sour cream with plain soy yogurt mixed with 1 teaspoon chili powder. Omit cheese or use soy cheese.*

Cheesy Yum Dip
Serves 4

For those who love Velveeta, this homemade version will hit the mark.

3 ounces (85 grams) cream cheese

½ cup (60 grams) shredded cheddar cheese

¼ cup (65 grams) chunky mild salsa (optional)

2 tablespoons milk

1. Combine cream cheese and cheddar cheese in a small saucepan; stir over low heat until melted. Stir in salsa and milk. Heat thoroughly, stirring occasionally.

2. Transfer to bowl and serve with tortilla chips, veggies, or use as a topping for noodles or baked potatoes.

Dairy-Free Variation: *Use soy cheddar and soy cream cheese. Use water in place of milk.*

 # Cucumber Yogurt Dip
Makes 2 cups (500 grams)

Serve this dip with veggies and tortilla strips.

2 cups (500 grams) plain yogurt

½ red onion, diced small

1 tablespoon each chopped fresh mint and coriander

1 cucumber, peeled and diced

1 teaspoon lemon juice

1 teaspoon each ground cumin and pepper

1. Mix all ingredients in a bowl and serve.

2. Refrigerate any unused portion—but eat within one day.

Dairy-Free Variation: *Use soy or goat yogurt.*

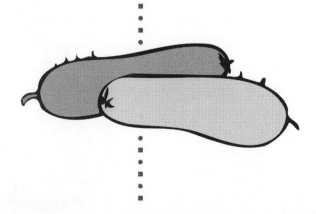

 ## Fuzzy Fruit Ambrosia
Serves 6

*This festive dish is great for parties—my family serves
it as a side dish on Thanksgiving—but we enjoy it as a
refreshing fruit salad snack throughout the year.*

1 15½-ounce (430-gram) can pineapple, drained

2 6-ounce (170-gram) cans mandarin oranges, drained

1 cup (170 grams) sliced fresh strawberries

1 12-ounce (340-gram) package shredded coconut

1 16-ounce (455-gram) tub sour cream

1. Mix all ingredients together in a large bowl. Cover and refrigerate for at least 2 hours before serving.

Dairy-Free Variation: *Use soy or goat yogurt in place of sour cream.*

Low-Sugar Variation: *Use unsweetened shredded coconut and/or omit tinned fruit, use fresh instead.*

GLUTEN may be not only making your child sick, but it may be also making you fat! Some researchers believe that grains like wheat, rye, and barley slow metabolism, suppressing fat burning and triggering binging. Dr. James Braly, MD, author of *Dangerous Grains,* says that when his patients give up grains, "the fat just melts off." You may be able to tell if gluten is making you fat by taking a simple test. Kits cost around $99.00 and are available at www.yorkallergyusa.com.

Crunchy Granola Bars
Makes 30

Use the crumbs of these bars for a yogurt parfait or chop up the whole batch for a delicious granola cereal. Try adding one cup into your favorite quick bread mix! The trick to making granola bars that stay together is to leave the bars untouched until totally cool. A friend of mine whose children love granola bars suggests leaving these covered on the counter overnight to make it easier to cut.

½ cup (125 grams) butter

⅓ cup (70 grams) sugar or honey

1 tablespoon light corn syrup or maple syrup

4 cups (400 grams) oats or buckwheat flakes

½ cup (75 grams) raisins (or favorite dried fruit)

⅓ cup (40 grams) chopped nuts (optional)

1. Lightly coat 8-inch square cake pan with cooking spray.
2. Place the butter, sugar, and syrup in a pan and cook over low heat, stirring until the mixture is well combined.
3. Remove the pan from heat and stir in the oats until coated. Add the fruit and nuts; mix well.
4. Turn into pan and press down firmly.
5. Bake in a 350°F (180°C) oven for 30 minutes. Cool for 30 minutes and then place in refrigerator. When completely cool, cut with a knife into bars.

Dairy-Free Variation: Use margarine.

Low-Sugar Variation: Omit all sugars, use ⅓ cup sugar-free maple syrup.

Nut-Free Variation: Omit nuts.

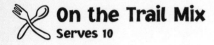

On the Trail Mix
Serves 10

Little hands love digging into this high-fuel snack, best offered on the go.

Crunchy Granola Bars recipe (page 37)
1 cup (70 grams) toasted coconut (optional)
1 cup (150 grams) chopped dried fruit
1 cup (180 grams) yogurt raisins
½ cup (15 grams) of your favorite rice or corn cereal
½ cup (75 grams) salted nuts (optional)

1. Crush granola into bite-size pieces and crumbs. Mix all ingredients. Keep in a large sealed plastic container. You may freeze this trail mix for up to 1 month.

Dairy-Free Variation: Omit yogurt raisins, use plain.

Low-Sugar Variation: Use unsweetened coconut. (Follow Low Sugar Variation in Crunchy Granola recipe, p. 37.)

Nut-Free Variation: Omit nuts.

NUT ALLERGY is an increasingly recognized problem, particularly in children. Whilst it has been recognized for decades, it is clear that the proportion of children affected has increased dramatically in recent years. Anaphylaxis is a word used for reactions to nuts of the type, which, if severe enough, can be life-threatening. Nut allergy can produce:

• A tingling feeling in the lips or mouth

• An itchy nettle rash (urticaria, hives), either where the nuts touch you, or elsewhere

• Swelling (angioedema), either where the nuts touch you, or elsewhere

• Swelling in the throat, causing difficulty in swallowing or breathing

• Asthma symptoms

• Vomiting

• Cramping tummy pains

• Diarrhea

• Faintness and unconsciousness

(Source: www.users.globalnet.co.uk)

"CAUTION: Do not feed honey to infants under 1 year old—bacteria, which can grow in unsterile products, can cause infant botulism. The same bacteria, however, will usually not affect older children and adults. Curiously, medical researchers in Africa have shown that honey can help clean burns and wounds, reducing the possibility of infection." (Source: *Prevention* magazine's *Nutrition Advisor*)

Cinnamon Crunch Snack Mix
Makes about 5 cups (200 grams)

My kids call this recipe the "ultimate snack."

2 tablespoons (30 grams) margarine

1 teaspoon sugar

2 teaspoons corn syrup, maple syrup, or honey

½ teaspoon ground cinnamon

4½ cups (135 grams) puffed rice or corn cereal

⅓ cup (50 grams) raisins or chopped dried fruit

⅓ cup (40 grams) nuts or coconut (optional)

1. In a microwave-safe bowl, melt margarine. Add sugar, syrup, and cinnamon; stir.

2. In a large bowl, mix the cereal, raisins, and nuts. Pour wet mixture over this mixture and toss until all is coated.

3. Pour onto a baking tray. Bake at 250°F (120°C) for about 15 minutes. Remove and stir. Let sit for 10 minutes and pour into a bowl to serve. You can store the leftovers in a zipper-lock bag or a covered container.

Low-Sugar Variation: Use 1 tablespoon of sugar-free maple syrup; use unsweetened coconut.

Nut-Free Variation: Omit nuts.

Honey Mustard Snack Mix
Makes about 5 cups (200 grams)

Tangy and sweet, this makes the perfect after-school snack. My husband and I enjoy munching on this during the few opportunities we get to sit and watch TV.

2 teaspoons oil

2 teaspoons Dijon-style mustard

2 teaspoons honey or corn syrup

4½ cups (135 grams) puffed corn or rice cereal

1 cup (150 grams) gluten-free pretzels or dried peas (optional)

1. In a large bowl, combine the oil, mustard, and honey. Add the cereal and pretzels. Stir to coat.

2. Bake at 250°F (120°C) for 15 minutes. Remove and stir. Let the snack mix sit for 10 minutes before serving.

Low-Sugar Variation: Omit syrup. Mix 2 teaspoons Whey Low with the oil.

WHENEVER YOU purchase a new product from the store—like crisps or pretzels—I highly recommend calling the customer service line and checking that, indeed, the offending ingredient isn't in the product. Ingredients are subject to change by the manufacturer. Most companies list toll-free consumer numbers somewhere on the packaging, making it simple to guarantee your child won't be eating something that could harm him. Incidentally, Ener-G Foods makes a great gluten-free pretzel.

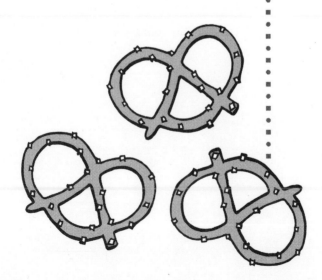

Cut Out Croutons
Makes about 2 cups (200 grams)

Try cutting these croutons into tiny squares for salads, soups, and snacks or use fun biscuit cutters to make giant crunchy treats for toddlers.

4 pieces gluten-free bread

½ cup melted butter or olive oil

2 teaspoons dried seasonings (parsley or basil)

¼ cup (40 grams) Parmesan cheese

Dash salt and pepper

1. Toast the bread in a toaster on medium-low heat 3 or 4 times until very dry. Do not let burn. Set aside to cool.

2. In a large bowl, stir together the butter, seasonings, and Parmesan.

3. Cut the toast into bite-size squares or into desired cookie-cutter cut-out shapes.

4. Add the toast shapes to the bowl and toss until each piece is seasoned. Add salt and pepper if desired.

5. Grease a baking tray and evenly space the croutons on the sheet. Bake at 350°F (180°C) for 5 minutes on each side. Remove and let cool on baking tray for 15 minutes. Serve or store in a covered container for up to 1 week. You may freeze these.

Dairy-Free Variation: *Omit Parmesan and use olive oil.*

Chewy Granola Bars
Serves 12

Although this recipe calls for chocolate chips, occasionally use white chocolate chips and dried apricots for a tangy and sweet combination.

1 cup (250 grams) butter

¾ cup (150 grams) brown sugar

½ cup (100 grams) sugar

2 tablespoons corn syrup or maple syrup

4 cups (400 grams) oats or buckwheat flakes

1 cup (70 grams) shredded coconut

⅓ cup (40 grams) chopped nuts

1 cup (175 grams) chocolate chips and/or your
    favorite dried fruit

1. Grease a 12-inch x 9-inch baking tray.

2. In a large pan, heat butter, sugars, and syrup until melted.

3. Stir in remaining ingredients until evenly combined.

4. Spread on baking tray and press down, making sure the surface is smooth.

5. Bake in a 325°F (170°C) oven for 30 minutes.

6. Cool for 20 minutes and then cut into bars. Transfer to a cooling rack and cool completely.

Dairy-Free Variation: *Use margarine.*

Nut-Free Variation: *Omit nuts.*

"BUCKWHEAT is a grain that has been eaten for hundreds of years in the Far East. China, Japan, Korea, and other Asian countries have long enjoyed noodles made from buckwheat flour. Buckwheat can also be used for a variety of baked products, including pancakes, breads, muffins, crackers, bagels, cookies, and tortillas among others. Buckwheat is thought of as a cereal, but is actually an herb of the buckwheat family, Polygonaceae."
(Source: www.specialfoods.com)

DO YOU KNOW what accounts for the hundreds of varieties of honey? The flavor of honey varies depending on the type of nectar (from the flowers!) collected by the bees. And although the store shelves stock "golden" colors of honey—clover honey—honey colors range from white to black to purple to even green.

Morning Bars
Serves 12

An ideal quick snack when you and the kids are on the go!

⅔ cup (100 grams) raisins or dried fruit pieces (apples, blueberries, or apricots)

½ cup (125 grams) butter

½ cup (175 grams) honey or corn syrup

4 cups (400 grams) rolled oats or buckwheat

¼ cup (30 grams) buckwheat flour, potato flour starch, or rice flour

1 teaspoon baking soda

½ cup (60 grams) chopped nuts (optional) or shredded coconut (optional)

1 cup (150 grams) dried fruit (blueberries, apricots, or apples)

1. Place ⅔ cup (100 grams) of dried fruit pieces in a food processor fitted with the metal blade and process until smooth, about 30 seconds. Add the butter and process until smooth. Add the honey and blend until smooth. Set aside.

2. In a large bowl, mix together oats, flour, and baking soda. Stir in the nuts and the dried fruit pieces. Pour the fruit-butter mixture into the oat mixture and stir until thoroughly combined. If needed, pour half of the mixture back into the processor and pulse several times.

3. Line a 9-inch × 13-inch baking pan with parchment. Press the mixture firmly and evenly into the pan. Bake for 30 minutes in a 325°F (170°C) oven. Remove and let cool for at least 4 hours. Invert onto a cutting board and lift pan to remove. Peel off the parchment paper. With a long, sharp knife, cut into desired granola bar sizes.

Dairy-Free Variation: Use margarine.

Low-Sugar Variation: Omit honey or corn syrup.

Nut-Free Variation: Omit nuts.

Mommy's Mock Goldfish Crackers
Serves 8

So many options exist with these easy, cheesy crackers. Stack them with other snack foods for a sandwich-type creation or fill them with peanut/soy/almond butter for a fun snack! This dough also works nicely for pizza bites and quiches.

2 cups (240 grams) shredded cheese (sharp cheddar, mozzarella, and soy cheese work well)

½ cup (125 grams) butter

1½ cups (185 grams) rice flour

¼ teaspoon salt

¼ teaspoon ground cayenne pepper

1. In a food processor, blend cheese and butter together.
2. Add remaining ingredients and blend until a ball forms and all ingredients are thoroughly combined.
3. Divide dough in half. You can flatten it into disks or roll it into a log. Cover with plastic wrap.

   For cracker shapes: Roll disk out to ¼ inch on a cutting board. Freeze dough for 10 minutes. Use biscuit cutters or let child roll into bread sticks. Make sure all crackers are even in size. Place on a lightly greased baking tray and bake at 350°F (180°C) for 15 minutes. Let crackers cool on a cooling rack.

   For cut crackers: Slice ¼-inch slices from chilled log. Bake according to above directions.
4. Store in sealed plastic container or freeze in a plastic freezer bag for 1 month. Uncooked dough may be kept frozen for 1 month.

   For Cheez-It-style crackers, sprinkle lightly with coarse salt while crackers are warm.

Dairy-Free Variation: *Use soy cheese or soy cream cheese and margarine.*

I CALL MYSELF the weekend baker! It takes a few days a week to prepare foods like muffins, mini-quiches, and mock Goldfish crackers and then freeze and package them. Once you get started, it is a breeze! I always look at my food preparation in a positive light, regardless of our allergies and my celiac disease. I feel truly blessed to know that my family is eating foods that I have prepared with love. No chemicals, low sugar, no preservatives—just gluten-free, allergy-free goodness! It takes more time to cook things that are so easy to buy—like casseroles and Twix bars—but the benefits are rewarding! My children love to participate in the process of preparing most of our snacks and treats. I see that their interest in making the foods makes them more inclined to try their new foods. This is especially true if you have a picky eater! Invite your children to scoop out the cookies or create their own pizza toppings. I often hear my oldest tell her friends at the park—who are usually eating store-bought Goldfish crackers—"Taste my cracker. I made it myself!" She is proud of her cooking talents and her wheat-free cracker, too.

WHEN A PARENT discovers that a child has an allergy to wheat, suddenly it seems like every food is off limits—so many of our packaged snacks and snack foods do include flour as a key ingredient. But many snack foods, like these deviled eggs, contain no gluten whatsoever. Part of feeding your child begins with taking a deep breath and recognizing all the wheat-free things we can eat!

Devilish Eggs
Serves 6

For a high-protein variation, try omitting the yolks and filling with Tuna-Fish Salad (p. 56) instead.

6 hard-boiled eggs
4 tablespoons mayonnaise
2 teaspoons rice vinegar
1 tablespoon mustard
1 tablespoon relish (dill or sweet), optional
Paprika for sprinkling
Dash salt and pepper

1. Remove shells from eggs and halve lengthwise.
2. Remove yolks and place in a bowl.
3. Mash yolks with next 3 ingredients until smooth.
4. Add relish and stir.
5. Fill each egg half with yolk mixture. Sprinkle with paprika and a dash of salt and pepper. Keep refrigerated. Serve immediately with pickle wedges.

Egg-Free Variation: Try the Vegan Salad (see page 57) and serve with chips.

Rice Cracker Personal Pizzas
Serves 6

Kids love creating their own personal pizzas. Just place all the ingredients in front of them and let them go for it!

6 rice or corn crackers

1 jar of premade pizza or marinara sauce

2 cups (240 grams) shredded cheese

1 8-ounce (225-gram) package of pepperoni slices

1 cup (125 grams) sliced veggies (pick your favorites)

⅓ cup (50 grams) Parmesan cheese

1. Place rice crackers on a baking tray and top with sauce, cheese, and toppings.
2. Bake in a 350°F (180°C) oven for 10 minutes or until cheese is melted.
3. Serve immediately.

Dairy-Free Variation: *Use soy cheese or try this snack without cheese.*

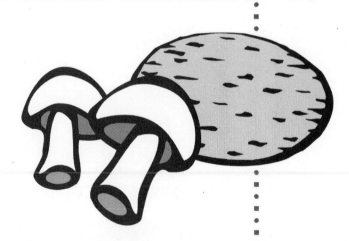

FORGET THAT old information warning nursing mothers to avoid garlic. Researchers at the Chemical Senses Center in Philadelphia, Pennsylvania, found that infants actually stayed at the breast longer and drank more milk when their mothers ate garlic! Way to go, stinking rose.

Bean Salad
Serves 8

Certainly a healthy snack, but this salad also makes a great side dish to any meal.

1 15½-ounce (430-gram) can each black beans, kidney beans, and garbanzo beans

1 small red onion, finely chopped

1 teaspoon chopped garlic

¼ cup chopped coriander

⅓ cup rice vinegar

1 tablespoon sugar (optional)

¼ cup light olive oil

2 teaspoons celery or poppy seeds

Salt and pepper to taste

1 12-ounce (340-gram) package frozen fancy green beans, defrosted

1. Drain and rinse all tinned beans; set aside.
2. In a large bowl, stir onion, garlic, coriander, vinegar, sugar, oil, seeds, salt, and pepper until combined.
3. Add tinned beans and green beans. Cover and refrigerate for at least 4 hours before serving.

Low-Sugar Variation: Omit sugar.

Go Cucumbers!
Makes 2 cups (200 grams)

Most parents have to struggle with their children to eat their vegetables, but with this yummy salad, my daughter, Allison, requests it often.

1 teaspoon salt

2 large English hothouse cucumbers, thinly sliced

½ cup (100 grams) sugar

1 cup rice vinegar

½ cup (30 grams) chopped fresh parsley

1 small red onion, thinly sliced

1. Sprinkle salt over cucumbers on a plate lined with a cotton kitchen towel and set aside.
2. Wisk sugar and vinegar in a large bowl. Add cucumbers, parsley, and onion. Toss together, cover, and refrigerate for 2 hours before serving.

Low-Sugar Variation: Use ¼ cup Whey Low in place of sugar.

CELIAC DISEASE—once thought rare—has recently been found to be more common, occurring in 1 in every 167 healthy children in the United States and 1 in every 111 healthy adults.

LACTOSE INTOLERANCE and milk allergies are not the same thing! Those with lactose intolerance lack the enzyme necessary to digest lactose (milk sugar) and should substitute dairy with products made from soy, rice, oats, grains, or nuts. Those with milk allergies react to the proteins found in milk and should avoid products with casein milk protein such as dairy-free cheeses.

Creamy Potato Salad
Makes 5 cups (1.3 kilograms)

Extra mayonnaise and sweet relish give this a deli-style kick that kids seem to love.

1½ cups (355 grams) mayonnaise

2 teaspoons mustard

Salt and pepper to taste

¼ cup (60 grams) sweet pickle relish

½ sweet white onion, finely chopped

2 celery stalks, finely chopped

2 hard-boiled eggs, chopped small (optional)

6 medium white potatoes, cooked, cooled, peeled, and cubed

Paprika for sprinkling

1. In a large bowl combine mayonnaise, mustard, salt and pepper, relish, onion, celery, and eggs. Gently fold in potatoes. Sprinkle with paprika. Cover and refrigerate for at least 2 hours.

Dairy-Free Variation: Use dairy-free mayo.

Egg-Free Variation: Use egg-free mayo and omit eggs.

Two Potato Salad
Makes 4 cups (1.1 kilograms)

This is a healthier and more colorful version of potato salad. Make it quickly by omitting oil and vinegar and adding your favorite non-allergy Italian salad dressing.

3 purple potatoes, cooked, cooled, and cubed

3 Yukon Gold potatoes, cooked, cooled, and cubed

½ red pepper, thinly sliced

½ red onion, thinly sliced

⅓ cup rice or red wine vinegar

¼ cup olive or vegetable oil

⅓ cup (20 grams) fresh chopped parsley

Salt and pepper to taste

¼ cup (40 grams) grated Parmesan cheese (optional)

2 tablespoons chopped fresh or dried basil

2 tablespoons chopped olives (optional)

1. Combine all ingredients in a bowl. Cover and refrigerate for at least 30 minutes. If using purchased dressing, omit the vinegar and oil.

Dairy-Free Variation: Omit Parmesan.

SO OFTEN we think of fruits packing the vitamin C punch—but one line of veggies offers a wallop of vitamin C. Peppers! Sweet green and red bell peppers both provide over 100 milligrams per serving—important information because vitamin C needs to be replenished every day. And sweet red peppers not only are loaded with vitamin C but also provide over 2,000 milligrams of vitamin A! These peppers may not prove hot to your senses, but they certainly are hothouses of vitamins.

Turkey Rice Salad
Makes 6 cups (1.5 kilograms)

Want to go vegetarian? Just omit the turkey! This is a fabulous dish to serve during the fall holidays.

2 cups (330 grams) steamed wild rice blend

1 cup (140 grams) diced cooked turkey or chicken

¼ cup (25 grams) chopped spring onions

½ small red onion, diced

½ cup (90 grams) chopped dried apricots or cranberries

¼ cup (30 grams) chopped red pepper (optional)

¼ cup (30 grams) finely chopped celery, including the leaves

4 tablespoons frozen orange juice concentrate, thawed

¼ cup rice vinegar

3 teaspoons sugar (optional)

2 teaspoons minced garlic

¼ cup (15 grams) chopped fresh parsley

¼ cup vegetable oil

1 teaspoon dried mustard

Salt and pepper to taste

1. In a large bowl combine cooled rice, turkey, onions, apricots, pepper, and celery.

2. In a small bowl mix remaining ingredients. Pour into large bowl and mix together. Refrigerate until ready to serve.

Low-Sugar Variation: *Replace orange juice concentrate with fresh squeezed juice.*

Rice Vinegar Asian Salad
Makes about 2 cups (250 grams)

Just because they're little doesn't mean they can't appreciate the tastes of the world! My children dig into this Asian-infused snack.

¼ cup rice vinegar

2 tablespoons oil

1 tablespoon minced peeled fresh ginger or 1 teaspoon dried ginger

2 teaspoons sesame oil

2 teaspoons honey

1 16-ounce (455-gram) bag prepared coleslaw cabbage

Cayenne or black pepper to taste

¼ cup (25 grams) sliced spring onions

1 tablespoon sesame seeds, toasted

½ cup (60 grams) crushed almonds or peanuts

1. In a large bowl mix together vinegar, oil, ginger, sesame oil, and honey.
2. Stir in cabbage mixture, pepper, and spring onions until thoroughly coated. Toss in sesame seeds and stir.
3. Sprinkle crushed nuts over top and serve.

Low-Sugar Variation: Omit sugar.

Nut-Free Variation: Omit nuts, sesame seeds.

TO MAKE mincing/grating gingerroot a (fragrant) breeze, a nifty tool can be purchased from Williams-Sonoma. The Porcelain Ginger Grater is made in Japan, where ginger is an essential ingredient. This porcelain grater is molded with teeth that quickly shred ginger's fibrous root. The shallow bowl collects the gratings and flavorful juices. A silicone ring underneath holds the grater in place. It measures 4¾ inches × 4¼ inches. This is a Williams-Sonoma exclusive and is $12.

CHECKING LABELS unfortunately becomes a requirement for parents of children with food allergies. If your child has wheat allergies, some items that you may not consider potential allergens can act that way because they indicate the presence of wheat protein: gelatinized starch, hydrolyzed vegetable protein, modified food starch, natural flavoring, soy sauce, vegetable gum, and vegetable starch.

Brown Rice and Apple Salad
Serves 5

In the summer, try adding 1 cup of sliced grapes, strawberries, and melon for a fruitier and cooler dish on a hot day.

2 tablespoons rice vinegar

2 tablespoons olive oil

1 tablespoon honey (optional)

Juice and zest of ½ orange

2 cups (330 grams) cooked, chilled brown rice

1 medium apple, chopped

1 cup (120 grams) sliced celery

⅓ cup (50 grams) currants

¼ cup (15 grams) chopped fresh parsley

¼ cup (60 grams) shelled sunflower seeds

1. In a large bowl mix vinegar, oil, honey, orange juice, and zest.
2. Stir in rice, apple, celery, currants, parsley, and sunflower seeds. Serve.

Low-Sugar Variation: Omit honey.

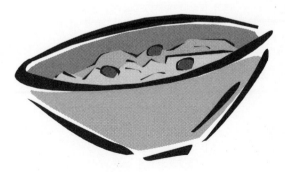

Salsa Bean and Rice Salad
Makes about 4 cups (800 grams)

Although this is packed with protein, it is a light dish. When I want to give my children a heavier snack to hold them over, I'll add shredded cheese.

1 cup (260 grams) prepared salsa

2 tablespoons chopped coriander

2 tablespoons rice vinegar

2 tablespoons chopped spring onions

2 cups (330 grams) cooked and cooled rice
(brown, white, or favorite mix)

1 cup (160 grams) corn (frozen, fresh, or tinned),
rinsed and drained

1 15½-ounce (430-gram) can pinto or black beans,
drained and rinsed

1 red pepper, chopped

1 cup (120 grams) cheese, shredded or cubed (optional)

1. In a large bowl blend salsa, coriander, vinegar, and spring onions.

2. Stir in rice, corn, beans, and pepper. Refrigerate for 30 minutes; then sprinkle with cheese and serve.

Dairy-Free Variation: Omit cheese.

WHAT KID doesn't love corn? Just ½ cup (80 grams) of corn offers your lads and lassies 90 International Units (IU) of vitamin A, 5 milligrams of vitamin C, 204 milligrams of potassium, and 38 micrograms of folate.

Macaroni Salad
Makes 4 cups (600 grams)

Macaroni salad has been a favorite of children for generations. Now, kids with wheat allergies can enjoy it, too, when mom uses wheat-free macaroni or rice noodles.

1 12-ounce (340-gram) box elbow macaroni
   or penne rice noodles

1 cup (235 grams) mayonnaise

¼ cup (60 grams) sweet pickle relish

2 stalks celery, diced

1 small white onion, finely chopped

1 teaspoon prepared mustard

1 teaspoon rice vinegar

1. Prepare noodles according to package directions. Cool noodles completely.
2. In a large bowl combine all ingredients and mix well. Refrigerate until ready to serve.

Egg-Free Variation: Use egg-free mayo.

Gluten-Free Variation: Use gluten-free macaroni in place of regular macaroni, or the rice noodles.

 **Tuna-Fish Salad**
Serves 5

I serve this tuna salad on a bed of lettuce with tortilla chips. It's fun for the kids to dip the tortilla chips in the salad, and I'm happy because they're getting a helping of a low-fat protein.

⅓ cup (80 grams) mayonnaise

¼ cup (35 grams) finely diced onion

2 tablespoons sweet or dill relish

1 tablespoons prepared mustard

½ small cucumber, diced

⅓ cup (50 grams) diced tomatoes

¼ cup (15 grams) fresh chopped parsley

Squeeze of lemon

Salt and pepper to taste

2 6-ounce (170-gram) cans albacore tuna, drained

1. In a medium-size bowl, mix all ingredients together except the tuna. Add tuna last and stir.

Egg-Free Variation: *Use egg-free mayo.*

MANY PARENTS worry when their child suffers from a dairy allergy that that child won't receive enough calcium. Calcium, however, is best used by the body with magnesium, and while dairy products are rich in calcium, they offer little magnesium. In order for our bodies to use calcium for bone and tooth health, it must be balanced by magnesium. Foods that give the best ratio of calcium to magnesium usually don't cause allergic reactions! They are green, leafy vegetables like cabbage, brussels sprouts, broccoli, and spinach. If your child doesn't suffer from a nut allergy, nuts are also a great source of balanced calcium and magnesium.

DID YOU KNOW that there are about thirty proteins in cow's milk that can cause allergic reactions? The main protein culprit is casein. Casein is a large molecule designed for baby cows—not baby humans. Once in the stomach, casein molecules coagulate into a large, hard-to-digest lump, thus giving your infant or child tummy troubles.

Vegan Salad
Makes 1 cup (150 grams)

Like the tuna salad, I serve this on a bed of lettuce and let the kids scoop it with tortilla chips.

⅓ cup (80 grams) egg-free mayonnaise

¼ cup (35 grams) diced red onion

¼ cup (30 grams) each red and green pepper

1 teaspoon prepared mustard

½ small cucumber, diced

1 large carrot, chopped small

⅓ cup (50 grams) diced tomatoes

¼ cup (15 grams) fresh chopped parsley

Squeeze of lemon

Salt and pepper to taste

1. Add all ingredients in a medium bowl. Stir gently. Serve.

# Noodle Doodle Salad
Makes about 4 cups (600 grams)

Make this snack salad for your little ones when you know it'll be awhile between meals. It'll fill them up and keep them hunger-free for hours.

Macaroni Salad recipe, prepared (page 55)
1 cup (130 grams) frozen peas
¼ cup (30 grams) chopped pepper
1 6-ounce (170-gram) can tuna, drained (or chopped chicken or ham)

1. Mix all ingredients together and serve immediately.

Egg-Free Variation: *Use egg-free mayo.*

ACCORDING TO studies done by the U.S. Department of Agriculture, most kids don't eat a healthy, balanced diet rich in fruits and veggies. Although dietary guidelines recommend that children over two years of age eat five to nine servings of fruits and vegetables a day, fewer than 15 percent of grammar school children eat five or more servings and over half of all elementary age children don't eat any fruit at all on a given day. Those children missing out on the servings also miss out on important vitamins and minerals necessary for proper growth.

INTERESTED IN more information about gluten-related topics, including links to the latest research and articles on gluten intolerance? Navigate online to www.gluten-free.org.

Thai Rolls
Serves 8

Though more time consuming to prepare than most recipes in this book, these Thai Rolls make fabulous hors d'oeuvres for a party and are the perfect size for little hands, too.

⅓ cup (50 grams) finely chopped onion

1 teaspoon minced garlic

1 tablespoon (15 grams) butter or margarine

1 cup chicken broth or coconut milk

2 tablespoons cornstarch

½ teaspoon curry paste

2 cups (330 grams) Thai rice or wild rice, cooked

¼ cup (30 grams) chopped peanuts or almonds

8 rice paper wrappers

½ cup (60 grams) each carrots and mange-tout, cut into thin strips

1. In a small saucepan cook onion and garlic in the butter for 3 minutes.

2. In a small bowl whisk broth, cornstarch, and curry paste. Stir into hot onion mixture. Cook and stir until thickened, about 5 minutes. Set ⅔ cup sauce aside.

3. Combine rice, nuts, and sauce in a large bowl.

4. Dip each rice paper in warm water and place between paper towels. Let stand for 10 minutes, set aside.

5. Steam veggies for 2 minutes.

6. To assemble each roll, take 1 rice paper and fill with 2 tablespoons of rice mixture. Place each carrot and pea pod over rice. Fold rice paper over on each side. Roll up as you would a burrito. Repeat.

7. In a steamer, place roll seam-side down and steam for 5 minutes. Serve with reserved dipping sauce.

Nut-Free Variation: *Omit nuts.*

Spring Rolls
Serves 16

Though rice papers are traditionally used in spring rolls, the wee ones seem to love the large lettuce leaf version instead. Let your kids decide!

4 ounces (115 grams) rice noodles, preferably vermicelli

1 cup (75 grams) packaged coleslaw salad cabbage mix

⅓ cup (40 grams) crushed almonds or peanuts

3 tablespoons chopped coriander

1 tablespoon oyster sauce

1 tablespoon tamari

1 tablespoon sesame oil

16 8-inch round rice papers or cleaned large lettuce leaves

⅓ cup hoisin sauce

¼ cup (65 grams) plum sauce (or plum jam)

2 teaspoons water

1. Cook rice noodles according to directions. Chop noodles into short pieces.
2. In a large bowl mix together cabbage, noodles, and nuts.
3. In a small bowl combine coriander, oyster sauce, tamari, and oil. Pour over noodle mixture and toss.
4. Dip rice papers in warm water one at a time and lay on paper towels. Let stand for 10 minutes.
5. Spoon about 3 tablespoons of noodle mixture onto each rice paper. Tightly roll filled rice paper up from bottom, tucking in opposite sides as you roll. Repeat for each paper.
6. In a small bowl mix hoisin sauce, plum sauce, and water. Serve as dipping sauce.

Nut-Free Variation: *Replace sesame oil with olive oil and omit nuts.*

MMMMMM—our families love plum sauce. Plums are a great source of fiber and rich in vitamin A and potassium. So let the little ones dip away at the tangy sauce that's all fruit.

Rice Snowballs
Serves 10

My only problem with these is that I keep eating them as I go along!

3 tablespoons rice vinegar

1 tablespoon sugar (optional)

4 tablespoons tamari

3 cups (500 grams) steamed small white rice

1 tablespoon sesame oil

3 tablespoons sliced spring onions

2 courgette, chopped small

2 carrots, chopped small

2 tablespoons toasted sesame seeds

1. In a small frying pan combine vinegar, sugar, and tamari. Bring to a boil until sugar is dissolved; remove from heat. Pour over the steamed rice, stir, and set aside.

2. In the small frying pan add oil, spring onions, courgette, and carrots. Cook until carrots are tender, about 5 minutes. Set aside.

3. To form a ball, scoop about 2 tablespoons of rice mixture and form into a ball. Using your thumb, make an indentation, and fill with 1 teaspoon of vegetable mixture. Cover with rice mixture and gently squeeze with hands, dip into toasted sesame seeds. Cover and refrigerate until ready to serve. You may dip in tamari sauce or enjoy them plain.

Low-Sugar Variation: Omit sugar.

Nut-Free Variation: Replace sesame oil with olive oil and omit sesame seeds.

Rice Pinwheels
Serves 10

*For some reason, calling these "Pinwheels" and not
"Sushi" sounds more appealing to my three-year-old.
This is incredibly easy to prepare, so don't be intimidated.
I'll walk you through step-by-step.*

6 large nori sushi papers

2 cups (330 grams) steamed small white rice

1 small cucumber, peeled and sliced thin lengthwise

1 small avocado, sliced thin

½ cup tamari

½ cup rice vinegar

2 tablespoons sliced green onion

⅛ teaspoon prepared wasabi (optional)

1. In a large dry frying pan on medium heat, place 1 nori paper
   in frying pan and let toast until sides start to curl or when nori
   becomes "neon." Make sure not to burn it. Flip over and toast
   the other side. Repeat with each paper.

2. Fluff rice with a fork. Place one paper down on a dry cutting
   board and firmly pat rice down until it covers all of the nori
   paper. If your hands get sticky, wet them with warm water.

3. Lengthwise from left to right, from side nearest to you, about
   3 inches in, place cucumber and avocado across filling to edges.

AFTER A SNACK or meal, moms
everywhere may give the little tykes a
bath. But did you know that if your child
suffers from a wheat allergy, labels
you'll want to read include shampoos,
bubble baths, and body gels. Many of
these products contain wheat and
gluten in their ingredients and can
cause an allergic reaction on the skin of
a sensitive child.

4. From side nearest you, flip the roll over the filling and firmly tuck in. Continue rolling, keeping the sides equal. You should have all of the rice and filling inside and only the nori paper showing. Flatten slightly with rice seam down.

5. With a very sharp, wet knife, slice roll at an angle, wiping blade off with a wet towel every other time. You may slice thin or thick depending on your preference.

6. Combine the last four ingredients in a small bowl. Place the bowl in the center of a plate and arrange sushi, lying flat, around it.

Variation: Try hollowing out a large cucumber and stuffing it with a mixture of rice, chopped avocado, and some of the cucumber leftovers. Slice into 2-inch pieces and serve with dipping sauce.

 **Ubu**
Serves 12

4 cups water

3 vegetable bouillon cubes

½ cup (160 grams) maple syrup

¼ cup tamari

24 tofu wrappers* (dried bean curd sheets)

1 small courgette, chopped small

1 carrot, peeled and diced small

½ white onion, chopped small

2 tablespoons sesame oil

2 cups (330 grams) steamed white rice

2 tablespoons toasted sesame seeds

1. Bring 4 cups water and vegetable cubes to a boil and turn heat to medium. Add in syrup and tamari. Place tofu wrappers in and let cook for about 30 minutes, in a covered pot.

2. Once papers appear that you could tear them in half (you may test them), remove from pot and let them drain and cool on paper towels.

3. Meanwhile, in a large frying pan, sauté courgette, carrot, and onion in the sesame oil for 3 minutes. Add steamed rice and sesame seeds. Remove from heat and set aside to cool.

4. Take a tofu wrapper and open a slot in the center, like a pillow-case. Try not to tear the sides. There should be 3 closed sides and 1 open.

5. Stuff rice mixture inside. They look like little footballs when they are finished.

*You can find the dried tofu wrappers at an Asian food market.

Low-Sugar Variation: Use sugar-free maple syrup or ½ cup Whey Low.

Nut-Free Variation: Replace sesame oil with olive oil and omit sesame seeds.

MEDICAL epidemiologists at the Centers for Disease Control believe that children who suffer from autism spectrum disorders have a genetic predisposition—basically a biological reason. But that the "biomarker" or "biological fingerprint" that autistic children possess must be somehow triggered by a pollutant or irritant. Since so many autistic children experience gastrointestinal problems, there are many people who believe that the "trigger" for some children is gluten or wheat. Although no study has yet proven this to be the case, the CDC is funding a study looking at the prevalence of autism and the possibility of food allergies as a cause. Regardless, many parents of autistic children who choose to modify their children's diets say that following a gluten-free diet saved their child's life.

Baked Potato Nachos
Serves 4

You can make these individually or increase the recipe for a roomful of hungry snackers.

1–2 baking potatoes

¼ cup (30 grams) shredded cheese

2 tablespoons chopped spring onions

1 small firm tomato, chopped

1. Place clean potatoes in the microwave (follow manufacturer's instructions for microwaving potatoes, usually about 5 minutes).

2. Working very carefully not to burn your fingers, slice the potatoes into long spears. I use a clean towel to hold the hot potato with. Arrange the potatoes in rows on a baking tray. Broil the potatoes for about 5 minutes, or until a little crispy. Remove from oven and sprinkle with cheese, spring onions, and the chopped tomato. Return to the grill for an additional 5 minutes or so. Make sure to watch so nothing burns. Remove with a spatula and place potatoes around a bowl of Guacamole Salsa or your favorite dipping sauce. My kids like plain catsup with this.

Dairy-Free Variation: *Omit cheese.*

Guacamole Salsa
Serves 4

⅓ cup (90 grams) prepared salsa

2 tablespoons sour cream

1 firm, ripe avocado

1. To make the guacamole, mix the salsa with the sour cream until blended. You can cut the avocado into small chunks and stir into the salsa, or you can mash the avocado into the salsa mixture.

Dairy-Free Variation: *Use soy yogurt.*

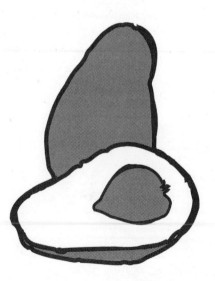

WANT TO EXPOSE your child to foods of the world? One way to do that is practice words used by other languages to describe various foods. A French example could include the word crudités:

Pronunciation: kr[UE]-dE-tA, krü-di-'tA

Function: noun plural

Etymology: French, from plural of crudités ("rawness"), from Latin cruditas ("indigestion"), from crudus

Date: 1960

Definition: pieces of raw vegetables (such as celery or carrot sticks) served as an hors d'oeuvre often with a dip. (Source: www.m-w.com)

It can make foods a fun geography and language opportunity!

WHEN THIS BOOK was being conceptualized, Leslie Hammond went out to various schools and surveyed children. She asked them what their favorite foods were. Overwhelmingly, the kids responded, "Pizza, nachos, and macaroni and cheese," as among their top favorites. Unfortunately for a kid with food allergies, all three are toxic to his or her little system. That's why Leslie felt compelled to find ways to feed little mouths their favorite foods—without causing an allergic reaction. Bon Appetit!

Pizza Bites
Serves 24

These may be kept frozen and reheated individually.

1 recipe Perfect Pie Crust (page 203)
1 10-ounce (280-gram) jar pizza sauce
16 ounces (455 grams) mozzarella cheese
1 8-ounce (225-gram) package pepperoni, chopped small
1 cup (125 grams) of your favorite toppings, chopped small
Grated Parmesan cheese for sprinkling

1. In mini or large muffin tins, place a scoop of dough and push around the sides and the bottom of the tin. Bake in a 350°F (180°C) oven for 10 to 15 minutes until golden and firm. Do not turn off the oven.

2. Remove from oven and fill with pizza sauce, cheese, pepperoni, and your favorite toppings. Sprinkle Parmesan cheese over the top.

3. Bake in the oven for about 10 more minutes. Cool almost completely and remove with a spoon. Serve, or cool for an additional 10 minutes and then place on a baking tray and put into the freezer for 30 minutes. Remove pizzas and place into a freezer zipper-lock bag and freeze up to 1 month. Remove and place directly into preheated oven at 350°F (180°C) on a baking tray, cook for 20 minutes. Or place in a microwave and cook on high for 3–6 minutes.

Dairy-Free Variation: Omit cheese.

Mexican Pizza
Serves 3

Store-bought tostadas make this an easy, inexpensive, and totally pleasing snack.

6 corn tortillas or tostadas

1 15½-ounce (430-gram) can refried beans

1 cup (260 grams) mild red enchilada sauce

1 cup (120 grams) shredded jack cheese

¼ cup (40 grams) chopped tomatoes

½ cup (60 grams) shredded cheddar cheese

¼ cup (25 grams) chopped spring onions

1. If using the corn tortillas, bake at 350°F (180°C) for 10 minutes or until firm.
2. Place 3 tortillas or tostadas on a greased baking tray. Spread beans on each tortilla. Top with remaining 3 tortillas.
3. Pour sauce on each tortilla. Top with jack cheese and tomatoes. Sprinkle each pizza with cheddar cheese and spring onions. Bake in a 350°F (180°C) oven for 30 minutes. Cut into fourths and serve.

Dairy-Free Variation: Omit cheese, or replace with soy cheese.

CHILDREN BETWEEN the ages of two and seven need 600 milligrams of calcium a day. Cheese, for those without dairy intolerances, is a great way to get both calcium and protein in one's diet. A small handful of shredded cheddar cheese provides about 200 milligrams of calcium. For kids with or without dairy allergies, try Nature's Plus Animal Parade Flavored Calcium Chewables—made from spinach, broccoli, and figs. They are good for mommies too!

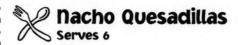 # Nacho Quesadillas
Serves 6

Make this a meal by adding your favorite meat.

1 cup (260 grams) Cheesy Yum Dip (see p. 34)

1 15-ounce (420-gram) can black beans,
  drained and rinsed

½ cup (130 grams) mild chunky salsa

6 corn tortillas

1. Heat all ingredients except tortillas in a saucepan over medium-low heat.

2. In a frying pan, over medium heat, place one tortilla down, add some filling, and top with a second tortilla. Cook both sides until tortillas are golden. Cut into triangles and serve.

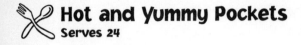

Hot and Yummy Pockets
Serves 24

1 cup water

½ cup (125 grams) butter

1 teaspoon sugar

½ teaspoon salt

2 cups (250 grams) rice flour

5 eggs

1 cup (260 grams) spaghetti sauce

½ cup (75 grams) Parmesan cheese

1 cup (125 grams) finely chopped broccoli,
   ham, or pepperoni

1. In a saucepan combine water, butter, sugar, and salt. Bring to a boil. Immediately stir in the flour. Return to heat and stir constantly to dry out the dough a bit for about 3 minutes.

2. Transfer the dough to your mixer. With your paddle attachment, mix on low speed to cool the dough for about 2 minutes. Add the eggs one at a time until smooth.

3. Push the dough into a large zipper-lock bag with the tip cut off, or a pastry bag. On a parchment or foil-lined baking tray, pipe out 2- to 4-inch balls.

4. Place into a 425°F (220°C) oven to puff the dough for about 10 minutes. Turn the heat down to 350°F (180°C) and bake an additional 15 minutes. Remove from oven to a cooling rack. Repeat heating directions with remaining dough.

5. Mix together the sauce, cheese, and broccoli, ham, or pepperoni. Place in a zipper-lock bag with a medium-size tip cut off the side.

6. To fill you may poke a hole in the bottom of the puff. Fill with mixture. If desired, roll ball in additional Parmesan cheese.

7. Bake in a 350°F (180°C) oven for 10 minutes, cool, and pop away! If wanting to freeze, omit baking and place in storage bag. Keeps frozen well for 1 month. Simply place on baking tray and bake at 350°F (180°C) for 15 minutes and serve.

Dairy-Free Variation: *Replace butter with margarine. Omit cheese.*

 **Mini Quiches**
Serves 24

These are great because they are a high-protein snack that can be kept frozen and used when needed. I make these in mini muffin tins.

3 eggs

½ cup half-and-half

¼ teaspoon each salt and pepper

1 recipe the Perfect Pie Crust (page 203)

1½ cups (180 grams) shredded cheese

½ cup (60 grams) chopped cooked ham
   or bacon (optional)

1 cup (150 grams) sautéed chopped veggies
   like mushrooms or broccoli

1. In a bowl, mix together the eggs, half-and-half, salt and pepper.

2. Take a pinch of dough and push it into the bottoms of the mini muffin or regular-size muffin tin. Put a little of each cheese, meat, and veggies in the muffin tins. With a ladle, spoon the egg mixture into each tin. Fill completely. Bake in a 350°F (180°C) oven for about 15 minutes or until the center of the egg mixture is firm. Remove and let cool to room temperature before serving.

3. To freeze, place in the refrigerator to completely chill. Place little quiches on a baking tray and put in the freezer for about 30 minutes. When they are able to hold their shape, put all of them in a freezer bag to freeze. They can be frozen for up to 2 months. To reheat, just place in the microwave for 1 minute, or until hot.

Dairy-Free Variation: *Replace half-and-half with ½ cup rice milk and omit cheese.*

Egg-Free Variation: *Use 3½ tablespoons of Ener-G Egg Replacer creamed together with ½ cup half-and-half or substitution.*

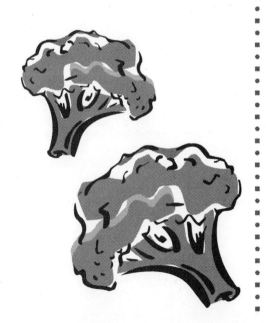

Puffy Potatoes
Serves 24

This also works well as a reheat-and-go snack.

6 medium potatoes, peeled and cubed

¼ cup (35 grams) chopped onion

3 tablespoons butter

¼ cup (30 grams) toasted gluten-free bread
    or cracker crumbs

¼ cup (40 grams) grated Parmesan cheese

1 teaspoon baking powder

Salt and pepper to taste

2 eggs, beaten

1. Cook potatoes for 25 minutes until tender.

2. Meanwhile, in a small pan cook onion in butter until tender.
   Set aside. Drain potatoes and mash until smooth. Add onion
   mixture, bread crumbs, Parmesan cheese, baking powder, salt
   and pepper. Beat in eggs.

3. On a well-greased baking tray, drop 10 mounds and bake
   uncovered in a 425°F (220°C) oven for 15 minutes. Serve
   with catsup or your favorite dip.

4. To freeze, cool completely and place in a freezer zipper-lock
   bag. Reheat individually in microwave or in oven until thoroughly heated.

Dairy-Free Variation: *Replace butter with margarine.*

Egg-Free Variation: *Omit eggs and mix 2 eggs' worth of Ener-G
Egg Replacer with water.*

THOUGH WHEAT may cause allergies, potatoes—long the staple and "staff of life" for the Irish—make a great starchy base from which to work and cook. The potato, in fact, may be a near perfect food. According to the U.S. Department of Agriculture, "A diet of whole milk and potatoes would supply almost all of the food elements necessary for the maintenance of the human body." Though 99.9 percent fat-free, spuds are nutrient dense and an important dietary staple in over 130 countries.

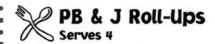

WHAT? ALLERGIC TO KISSING? According to the June 14, 2002, *Sacramento Bee*, people with food allergies may have to think twice before kissing—especially kissing someone who has recently eaten a food to which they are allergic. In most cases, the paper reported that "reactions were mild causing swelling and itching in the area kissed; however, a 3-year-old boy whose mother kissed him on the cheek after tasting pea soup, experienced a reaction so severe that he was rushed to the emergency room." This recipe, therefore, should be avoided by anyone with nut allergies.

PB & J Roll-Ups
Serves 4

We like to pack these for picnics and school lunches.

¾ cup (180 grams) favorite nut butter
¾ cup (240 grams) jam or honey
4 pancakes or crepes

1. Spread equal amounts of nut butter and jam down the center of each pancake.
2. Tuck the bottom in and roll together. Wrap in wax paper. Eat like a burrito.

Low-Sugar Variation: Use whipped fruit butter.

Nut-Free Variation: Omit peanut butter and use butter or cream cheese, if desired.

Courgette Sticks
Serves about 6

You can batter up almost any thing with this. I use this recipe for my tempura veggies and shrimp.

1 egg

1 cup milk or water

½ cup (60 grams) rice flour

½ cup (60 grams) cornstarch

1 teaspoon baking powder

Pinch of salt

2 cups (250 grams) courgette, onions, sweet potato, or any favorite veggie

1. Slice vegetable into long, slender spears. If making onion rings, cut into ¼-inch-thick slices and separate the rings.

2. In a large pot, heat 2 inches of oil to 325°F (170°C).

3. In a medium bowl, whisk together the egg and milk. Add the flour, starch, baking powder, and salt.

4. Dip the vegetable pieces into the batter. With a slotted metal spoon, lower the veggies into the oil. You can fry 3 to 4 at a time. Remove when golden. Set on a paper towel to drain. Serve.

Egg-Free Variation: Use 1 teaspoon Ener-G Egg Replacer with 1 teaspoon oil. Add to batter.

SQUASHES—like courgette—are indigenous to the Americas and belong to the family of curcurbita. Archaeologists have traced their origins to Mexico, dating back from 7,000 to 5,500 B.C., where the plant was an integral part of the ancient diet, along with corn and beans. Explorers brought back the strange vegetable, squash, to Europe; in fact, in Italy, it was named zucchino, a derivative of our English, "courgette." No matter what you call it, courgette offers valuable antioxidants and is rich in potassium.

 **Cheesy Rice Balls**
Serves 16

These cheesy rice balls are a popular appetizer in Italy.

2 cups (330 grams) arborio rice, cooked

2 tablespoons (30 grams) butter

⅓ cup (50 grams) grated Parmesan cheese

Salt and pepper

1 egg yolk

1 cup (132 grams) mozzarella cheese, cubed

1 egg, beaten

1½ cups (175 grams) fine gluten-free bread crumbs

Oil for frying

1. In a large bowl mix hot cooked rice, butter, Parmesan, and salt and pepper. Let cool.

2. Stir egg yolk into cooled rice mixture. Add mozzarella pieces and stir in. Form into balls the size of an egg. Roll each ball in beaten egg and coat with bread crumbs.

3. Heat 1 inch of oil in a deep frying pan. Fry balls until golden brown, turning occasionally. Drain well on paper towels. Serve warm with prepared marinara or ranch dressing as dipping sauce.

4. This does not work as well reheated. Eat that day.

Dairy-Free Variation: Omit cheeses and add 1 cup shredded courgette to rice.

Egg-Free Variation: Use 2 eggs' worth of Ener-G Egg Replacer and water. Roll each rice ball in mixture.

Polenta Snack Cakes
Serves 16

This is a great vegetarian dish that you can take with you when you are going places where you are unsure if the food is gluten-free, and these snack cakes taste great hot or cold.

1 16-ounce (455-gram) box 5-minute instant polenta

1 15½-ounce (430-gram) can black beans, drained and rinsed

1 15½-ounce (430-gram) can corn, drained and rinsed

½ cup (60 grams) each diced red pepper and red onion

2 cups (240 grams) shredded cheese

¼ cup (25 grams) chopped green onion

2 teaspoons chili powder

1 small courgette, shredded

1. Follow cooking instructions for quick-style polenta. Stir in all ingredients and pour into a large baking dish or greased muffin tin.
2. Bake in a 350°F (180°C) oven for 1 hour until firm, or 30 minutes for the muffins. Let cool for 30 minutes until firm and either cut into snack cakes or remove from muffin tins. Let cool completely. Cover and keep refrigerated for 5 days. They may be eaten cold or reheated.

Dairy-Free Variation: If the package of polenta calls for butter and milk, simply replace with equal amounts of oil and water. Use cheese substitute or omit.

OVERHEARD in a swank California bistro one evening was the alarmed, female Texas drawl, "Oh, my gosh, they are serving me grits!" Grits and polenta are not exactly the same thing—although both come from corn. Polenta is usually a boiled yellow cornmeal, seasoned, while grits are made by drying white corn and treating it with certain chemicals before grinding. Recently, however, polenta has found its way to some of the most pricey tables in America as a main course, whereas grits have a reputation as a side dish in Southern homes that costs little to prepare.

MUFFINS FROM THE BAKERY

Kids love muffins! Designed to mimic bakery-style treats, these muffins are easy and delicious. Take one and go! I am sure you will be as pleased as I am with these. You have the choice of making mini or regular muffins, mini or regular loaves, or cakes (sliced into wedges).

SO OFTEN people think that the reaction to food allergies is gastrointestinal or involves respiratory problems. Many food allergies, however, manifest themselves through dermatitis and other eczemas. According to the National Institute of Allergy and Infectious Diseases, health care provider visits for contact dermatitis and eczemas are 7 million per year and seem to be increasing in prevalence.

Banana Bread
Serves 12

3 ripe bananas
1 cup (200 grams) sugar
½ cup (125 grams) butter
3 eggs
1 teaspoon vanilla
¼ teaspoon salt
1 teaspoon baking soda
¼ teaspoon cinnamon
2 cups (250 grams) rice flour
½ cup (60 grams) chopped pecans

1. In a food processor, blend bananas, sugar, butter, eggs, and vanilla. Add remaining ingredients and process until smooth.
2. Pour into desired baking pans and bake at 350°F (180°C) until firm—mini muffins: 6 minutes, regular tins: 10–15 minutes, mini loaves: 15 minutes, bread loaf: about 60 minutes.

Dairy-Free Variation: Use margarine.

Egg-Free Variation: Omit eggs and add 1 extra banana.

Low-Sugar Variation: Omit sugar or add ¼ cup (85 grams) honey or sugar substitute.

Nut-Free Variation: Omit pecans if a nut allergy exists.

Awesome Blueberries
Serves 14

The ingredients are incorporated differently than usual, producing a tender cakelike muffin.

4 ounces (115 grams) cream cheese

2 cups (250 grams) white rice flour

1¼ cups (300 grams) sour cream

2 teaspoons vanilla

3 eggs

1 tablespoon baking powder

½ teaspoon salt

¼ teaspoon ground cinnamon (optional)

1 cup (200 grams) sugar

2 cups (300 grams) blueberries

1. In a mixer, whirl the cream cheese on medium speed until it crumbles into pieces. Add the flour and mix on low; then increase to medium speed for 30 seconds. Add the sour cream, vanilla, and the eggs; mix well. Scrape down sides. Add the baking powder, salt, and cinnamon. Pour the sugar over and mix briefly. Remove from mixer and stir in the blueberries.

2. Fill muffin tins and bake in a 350°F (180°C) oven for 10 minutes or until firm. Let cool on a rack. Serve.

3. For blueberry scones, add to mixture 1 cup (125 grams) rice flour. Drop large mounds of dough onto baking tray and bake in a 375°F (190°C) oven for about 10 minutes.

Dairy-Free Variation: *Use soy cream cheese and substitute regular sour cream w/ toffuti sour cream or pureed silken tofu.*

Egg-Free Variation: *Use 3 eggs' worth of Ener-G Egg Replacer and water.*

BERRY WONDERFUL news here: In 2001, researchers from Indiana University and Ohio State University found that phytochemicals in red and black raspberries and strawberries inhibit the growth of colon and esophageal cancer cells in rats resulting from exposure to benzopyrene, a carcinogen found in tobacco smoke. While a similar study has not been conducted with humans, there are numerous studies that show that diets rich in fruits and vegetables help reduce the risk of stomach, lung, mouth, colon, and esophageal cancer by as much as 30 to 40 percent. Start fighting cancer early by filling little fists with big, sweet strawberries and luscious raspberries. Not only will your child's body love the phytochemical rush, but also there's nothing cuter than a little smiling face smeared with berry juice. Warning: Some children are very sensitive to berries and so should consume them only after the age of two.

Lemon Poppy Seed
Serves 12

You can change this muffin to a lemon berry delight simply by omitting the poppy seeds and adding fruit. Raspberry lemon is my favorite! It makes a lovely bundt cake.

½ cup (125 grams) butter

1 cup (200 grams) sugar

4 eggs

1¾ cups (215 grams) rice flour

2 teaspoons baking powder

⅔ cup (160 grams) sour cream

Grated rind of 1 lemon

4 tablespoons lemon juice

¼ cup (30 grams) poppy seeds, plus more for sprinkling

1. Blend butter and sugar until creamy. Add eggs and blend. Add remaining ingredients and mix well.

2. Spoon into desired baking dishes and sprinkle with additional poppy seeds if desired. Bake at 350°F (180°C) until firm:

   Mini muffins: 10 minutes

   Regular muffins: 15 minutes

   8-inch cake pan or bundt pan: 45 minutes

Variation: Omitting the poppy seeds turns these into delicious cupcakes—simply top with whipped cream and your choice of berries.

Dairy-Free Variation: Use oil in place of butter, and soy yogurt in place of sour cream.

Egg-Free Variation: Cream together 2 tablespoons Ener-G Egg Replacer and ⅛ cup water, add as you would the eggs.

Low-Sugar Variation: Use ½ cup (160 grams) Whey Low.

PB and Banana Chip
Serves 24

I omit the chocolate chips and the sugar and make this muffin at least once a week!

2 eggs

3 bananas

½ cup (100 grams) sugar

½ cup (120 grams) peanut butter

½ cup milk

2 cups (250 grams) rice flour

2 teaspoons baking powder

1 teaspoon baking soda

1 cup (90 grams) chocolate chips (optional)

1. In a food processor, add eggs, bananas, sugar, and peanut butter. Blend until smooth.
2. Blend together milk, flour, baking powder, and baking soda. Add chocolate chips and pulse twice.
3. Pour batter in your choice of tins and bake in a 350°F (180°C) oven—mini muffins: 8 minutes, regular muffins: 11–15 minutes, mini loaves: 10 minutes, bread loaves: 45 minutes

Dairy-Free Variation: Use rice milk.

Egg-Free Variation: Omit eggs and add 1 extra banana.

Low-Sugar Variation: Omit sugar.

Nut-Free Variation: Decrease milk by ¼ cup. Omit peanut butter.

Sweet Potato Cranberry Muffins
Serves 24

With or without frosting, these muffins are so wonderful!
I recommend the creamsicle frosting.

½ cup (100 grams) sugar (optional)

⅔ cup (150 grams) brown sugar

¾ cup oil

4 eggs

2 cups (420 grams) tan-skinned sweet potatoes, peeled,
 cooked, and mashed

3 cups (375 grams) rice flour

2 teaspoons baking soda

2 teaspoons baking powder

½ teaspoon salt

1 teaspoon ground ginger

1 teaspoon ground cinnamon

¾ cup (120 grams) dried cranberries

1. In a large mixing bowl, combine sugars and oil. Blend.
   Add the eggs and mashed sweet potatoes and blend
   until smooth. Stir in flour, baking soda, baking powder,
   salt, ginger, and cinnamon. Blend until smooth. Remove
   bowl from mixer and stir in cranberries.

2. Pour batter into paper-lined muffin tins and bake in a
   350°F (180°C) oven for 20 minutes or until firm.

3. Cool on a cooling rack and frost if desired. Store in a
   covered container in the refrigerator.

Egg-Free Variation: Omit eggs.

Low-Sugar Variation: Use 1 cup Whey Low.

Bran and Raisin
Serves 20

½ cup tinned crushed pineapple, ½ cup juice reserved

¼ cup (85 grams) molasses

1½ cups (150 grams) rice or oat bran

1 teaspoon vanilla

½ cup (75 grams) raisins

1 egg

½ cup (115 grams) sour cream or plain yogurt

¼ cup oil

½ teaspoon cinnamon

1 cup (125 grams) rice flour

1 teaspoon baking powder

½ teaspoon baking soda

½ teaspoon salt

1 carrot or apple, shredded (optional)

1. Strain the juice from a can of crushed pineapple until you get ½ cup. Combine the juice, pineapple, molasses, bran, vanilla, raisins, egg, the sour cream or yogurt, and the oil. Let sit for 10 minutes.

2. Combine the dry ingredients in a large bowl. Add wet ingredients and mix. Add the carrot and stir.

3. Line a muffin tin with muffin papers. Fill ¾ full and bake in a 400°F(200°C) oven for about 10 minutes or until firm.

Dairy-Free Variation: *Use soy yogurt.*

Egg-Free Variation: *Omit egg.*

Low-Sugar Variation: *Omit molasses and tinned pineapple. Replace with ½ cup Whey Low and ½ cup shredded courgette.*

IT IS BELIEVED that humans discovered raisins when they happened upon grapes drying on a vine. And although the ancient world long harvested from their vineyards, historians say that eleventh-century Crusader knights first introduced raisins to Europe when they returned home from Byzantium. Whether you like yours golden or dark, sweet and chewy raisins make an excellent healthy alternative to sweets for the little ones any day! Just remember: Anything sticky and sweet requires a thorough tooth-brushing after eating.

A GREAT DAIRY-FREE variation for 1 cup buttermilk is ½ cup soy yogurt, ½ cup rice milk, and 1 tablespoon lemon juice.

Very Berry
Serves 16

A berry in every bite!

¾ cup (150 grams) sugar

½ cup (125 grams) butter

3 eggs

1¾ cup (215 grams) white rice flour

2 teaspoons baking powder

½ teaspoon salt

⅔ sour cream (160 grams)

4 tablespoons buttermilk

1 cup (145 grams) blueberries

1 cup (145 grams) raspberries

1 cup (170 grams) chopped strawberries

1. With a mixer, cream together sugar and butter for 30 seconds.

2. Add eggs and cream for 1 minute.

3. Add rice flour, baking powder, salt, sour cream, and buttermilk. Blend for about 15 seconds.

4. Remove from mixer and gently fold in berries.

5. Fill paper-lined muffin tins to top. Do not overfill. Bake in a 375°F (190°C) oven for 15 minutes or until firm. Remove and cool.

Dairy-Free Variation: Replace butter with margarine and substitute soy yogurt for buttermilk (above, left) and sour cream.

Egg-Free Variation: Use 3 eggs' worth of Ener-G Egg Replacer and water.

Low-Sugar Variation: Use ½ cup Whey Low.

Jumbo Vanilla Cherry
Serves 6

Kids really enjoy these. They are equally delicious with or without the chocolate.

⅓ cup (85 grams) butter

¾ cup (150 grams) white sugar

2 eggs

⅔ cup (160 grams) plain or vanilla yogurt

2 teaspoons vanilla

5 tablespoons milk

2 cups (250 grams) rice flour

1 teaspoon baking soda

⅔ cup (100 grams) frozen cherries

1 cup (90 grams) chocolate or white chocolate chips (optional)

1. Line 6 jumbo muffin tins with papers.
2. In a mixer, cream butter and sugar until light and fluffy. Beat in eggs, yogurt, vanilla, and milk until thoroughly combined.
3. Add flour and baking soda and blend.
4. Stir in cherries by hand. Add chocolate chips if desired.
5. Fill jumbo muffin tins ¾ to the top with the batter. Bake in a 375°F (190°C) oven for 25 minutes. Cool for 10 minutes and turn muffins out on a wire rack to cool completely.

Dairy-Free Variation: Replace butter, yogurt, and milk with equal parts margarine, soy yogurt, and rice milk.

Egg-Free Variation: Use 2 eggs' worth of Ener-G Egg Replacer and water.

Low-Sugar Variation: Use ½ cup Whey Low in place of sugar and omit chocolate chips.

ONE CUP of cherries—beyond being incredibly tasty and sweet—provides 3 grams of fiber, 12 percent of what one needs daily. Interestingly, cherries also are packed with protein for a little fruit. Again, one cup offers eaters 2 grams of protein.

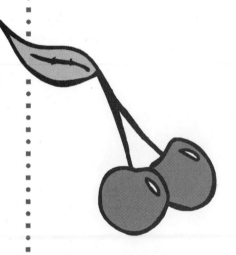

Vegan Tropical Muffins
Serves 16

These tasty, filling muffins are delightful with or without soy cream cheese frosting.

3–4 ripe bananas

2 cups (250 grams) rice flour

2 teaspoons baking powder

1 teaspoon baking soda

1 cup (250 grams) crushed pineapple, undrained

1¼ cups (90 grams) shredded coconut

2 teaspoons orange zest

½ teaspoon salt

1 8-ounce (225-gram) package soy cream cheese

⅓ cup orange juice

1 banana, sliced

1. In a food processor add 3–4 bananas, flour, baking powder, soda, pineapple and juice, 1 cup coconut, orange zest, and salt. Process until smooth.

2. Pour into paper-lined muffin tins and bake in a 350°F (180°C) oven for 25 minutes. Remove to a cooling rack. In a clean food processor, add the package of soy cream cheese and orange juice; blend until smooth. When muffins are room temperature, frost and arrange thinly sliced bananas and shredded coconut over the top for decorations. Serve. If you are storing muffins, do not apply sliced bananas, top only with coconut.

Low-Sugar Variation: Use fresh chopped pineapple and unsweetened coconut.

Mini Scones with Maple Drizzles
Serves 24

½ cup (125 grams) butter

¼ cup (55 grams) brown sugar

3 cups (375 grams) rice flour

¼ cup (80 grams) maple syrup (optional)

1 tablespoon baking powder

1 teaspoon cinnamon

Dash of nutmeg

½ teaspoon salt

½ cup (115 grams) sour cream

2 eggs

1 cup (250 grams) tinned pumpkin or applesauce

Sugar for sprinkling (optional)

1 cup (150 grams) your choice: chopped apples, dried
cranberries, raisins, or nuts

1. In a food processor, add the butter (cut into pieces), brown
   sugar, and 1 cup of flour. Process until all combined. Add all
   remaining ingredients except for sugar for sprinkling and
   dried fruit or nuts and blend until smooth.

2. Scoop into a large bowl and stir in dried fruit or nuts.

3. On a floured surface, scoop out a handful-size portion of
   dough and form into a disk. Using a knife, cut into pizzalike
   triangles of equal size. Place little triangles on a greased baking tray. You may make an egg wash with one egg and a teaspoon of water, or you may leave plain or sprinkle with sugar.
   Bake in 375°F (190°C) oven for 20 minutes, depending on
   the size of your scones. They should be lightly golden on the
   bottom. Remove to a cooling rack. When cooled you may
   make a maple glaze with ½ cup (60 grams) powdered sugar
   and enough maple syrup to reach a desired consistency.
   Drizzle over scones and serve.

NOWADAYS, we so often use fake maple syrup on our pancakes. But there's nothing like the taste of true maple syrup. Native Americans actually considered maple syrup a necessary component of their diet.

Dairy-Free Variation: Replace butter with margarine or oil and replace sour cream with soy yogurt.

Egg-Free Variation: Omit eggs.

Low-Sugar Variation: Omit sugar and maple syrup.

Nut-Free Variation: Omit nuts.

MOST PARENTS of children who suffer from a gluten allergy know to avoid wheat, but there are many other sources of gluten that one might not even consider, which you may use in cooking. Soy sauce, alcohol, and some teas all contain gluten. Rye, barley, and oats are also off limits to the gluten-free child, although recent studies seem to indicate that oats may actually be okay. The reason oats may not be okay would be from cross-contamination with wheat in the mills.

Baby Biscotti
Makes 18

¼ cup (60 grams) butter

⅓ cup (70 grams) sugar (optional)

⅓ cup (115 grams) honey or molasses

1 teaspoon vanilla

3 eggs

2 cups (250 grams) rice flour

1½ teaspoons baking powder

¼ teaspoon baking soda

¼ teaspoon salt

1 cup (100 grams) oats, rice bran, or buckwheat flakes

1 cup (110 grams) finely shredded carrots

1 cup (70 grams) shredded coconut (optional)

½ cup (75 grams) raisins, blueberries, dried apricots, or dates

1. Either in a food processor or a mixer, add butter, sugar, honey, vanilla, and eggs. Mix well. Add flour, baking powder, soda, salt, oats, carrots, coconut, and raisins; mix or process until well combined.

2. On two greased baking trays, make four loaves, two on each baking tray.

3. Bake in a 325°F (170°C) oven for 40 minutes or until golden and firm. Remove from oven and let cool for 10 minutes. With a thin spatula, cut each loaf at an angle into long 2-inch strips. Remove each cookie and put, cut side down, on a new, greased baking tray. Bake for 10 minutes and then flip over, until you have reached desired crunchy consistency. If needed, bake 5 minutes more. Cool and store in a covered container for up to 1 week. They freeze well for up to 2 weeks.

Dairy-Free Variation: Use margarine or oil.

Egg-Free Variation: Replace eggs with ¼ cup applesauce.

MEALS

Ah! The nutritional mainstay of the day—meals. Part of being a parent is planning healthy meals for your children—a tough task when many of the foods that most people eat are toxic to your family and cause allergic reactions. I've gathered up the recipes for all my family's favorite meals and modified them all to meet the special needs of your family's diet.

Buttermilk Pancakes
Serves 10

When I surveyed kids about their favorite foods, pancakes ranked high. Enjoy these traditional buttermilk pancakes for breakfast with your wee ones and watch a few cartoons, too.

2 eggs

2 cups (250 grams) rice flour

2 tablespoons sugar

2 teaspoons baking powder

1 teaspoon baking soda

1 teaspoon salt

2 cups buttermilk

¼ cup (60 grams) butter

2 teaspoons vanilla

1. Beat the eggs in a mixer on medium speed until frothy. Add the remaining ingredients. Mix batter until it is smooth, about 1 minute.

2. Pour desired amount of batter into a hot greased frying pan. When pancake bubbles and is lightly golden on the bottom, flip it over with a wide spatula. Cook until golden on bottom and remove to a plate. Stack until you have used all the batter. These make great pancake shapes like hearts and letters.

Variation: *After pouring the batter into the skillet, drop a desired amount of blueberries onto the pancake, cook, flip, and serve.*

Dairy-Free Variation: *Replace 2 cups buttermilk with 1 cup soy yogurt, 1 cup rice milk, and 2 tablespoons lemon juice. Replace butter with margarine.*

Egg-Free Variation: *Omit eggs.*

Low-Sugar Variation: *Omit sugar.*

INTERESTED IN reading up about food sensitivity? A good resource is *Hidden Food Allergies: Finding the Foods that Cause You Problems and Removing Them from Your Diet* by Stephen Astor, MD (Avery Publishing).

Blue Pancake Crepes with Blue Applesauce and Honey Syrup

Serves 12

We call them "blue" pancakes, but sometimes they are purple, which the kids love! These cakes roll nicely. Use whichever filling you and your kids prefer in them.

½ cup (75 grams) blueberries or blackberries

1 cup (125 grams) rice flour

2 teaspoons baking powder

¼ teaspoon salt

2 eggs

¾ cup rice milk

2 tablespoons oil

2 cups (500 grams) Blue Applesauce (page 21)

1. In a food processor, mix all ingredients until smooth.

2. Pour into a hot greased frying pan. Make each pancake crepe size and fairly thin. When golden on bottom, flip and cook other side. Stack on a plate. Let them cool to room temperature before rolling them. You may put wax paper between them and put them in a freezer bag. They freeze well for 2 weeks or so. Toast them or microwave them at 30-second intervals. Serve with Honey Syrup (recipe follows on next page).

Egg-Free Variation: *Omit eggs.*

 # Honey Syrup
Serves 6

1 cup water
1 cup (200 grams) sugar
Dash cinnamon
¼ cup (85 grams) honey
1 tablespoon (15 grams) butter

1. In a medium saucepan, combine the water and sugar; bring to a boil over medium-high heat. Stir until thickened into syrup; this takes about 10 minutes. Remove from heat and stir in cinnamon, honey, and butter.
2. To make a Blue Pancake roll, take a cooled pancake; fill with Blue Applesauce; roll, placing seam-side down on a plate; and pour syrup over. Or, roll up pancake tightly and let child dip into little cups of Honey Syrup and applesauce.

Dairy-Free Variation: *Use margarine.*

Low-Sugar Variation: *Mix 1 stick of butter or margarine with ½ cup Whey Low, ½ cup water, and 2 teaspoons maple flavoring. Bring to a boil and serve.*

A GOOD PLACE to get literature on allergies and asthma is the Allergy and Asthma Network Literature at 800-878-4403.

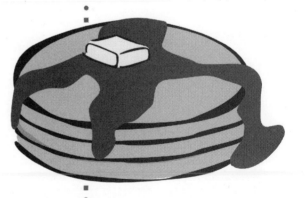

Pancake Torte
Serves 5

A yummy combination of a puffed pancake and an Impossible Pie. It makes its own crust and a delicious custard filling.

2 cups milk

¼ stick butter

1 cup (125 grams) rice flour

½ cup (100 grams) sugar

4 eggs

1 cup (200 grams) your choice: sliced peaches, apples, or shredded coconut

1. In a blender add the milk, butter, flour, sugar, and eggs. Blend until smooth. If using coconut, add it now.

2. Butter a 9-inch pie dish and arrange the sliced apples or peaches on the bottom. Pour the blended mixture over and bake in a 350°F (180°C) oven for 35 minutes. Cool slightly and slice like pie to serve. Good warm or cold.

Dairy-Free Variation: *Use soy milk and margarine.*

Low-Sugar Variation: *Replace sugar with ⅓ cup Whey Low and use fresh fruit or unsweetened coconut.*

French Toast Bake
Serves 8

This is bread pudding, but my girls insist that it tastes like French toast.

15 pieces gluten-free bread

4 eggs

3 cups milk

4 tablespoons melted butter

½ cup (100 grams) sugar

2 teaspoons vanilla

2 teaspoons cinnamon

1 cup (150 grams) raisins

1. Make sure the bread you use is firm and dry. To achieve a dry piece of toast, place it in the toaster on low heat several times until firm. Or leave the bread out a few days, loosely covered. Cut bread into cubes and set aside.

2. Whisk together the remaining ingredients except for the raisins. Grease a 12-inch × 8-inch baking dish. Place the bread cubes evenly in the baking dish and sprinkle with raisins. Pour the egg mixture over the bread. Place in a 350°F (180°C) oven for about 35 minutes. Let sit 10 minutes before serving. If desired, sprinkle with powdered sugar or cinnamon and sugar.

Dairy-Free Variation: Use soy milk and margarine.

Low-Sugar Variation: Use ½ cup Whey Low and omit raisins.

Breakfast Skillet
Serves 6

My children like to tear up the corn tortillas for me. They call this dish the "Messy Breakfast Burrito."

1 tablespoon olive oil

1 small onion, chopped

3 corn tortillas, torn into 1-inch pieces

1 firm ripe tomato, diced (optional)

5–6 eggs

¼ cup (65 grams) salsa

1 cup (120 grams) shredded cheese

1 avocado, sliced

1. In a medium frying pan with a lid, heat olive oil and onion and cook for 1 minute over medium heat. Add tortillas and tomato; cook about 2 minutes longer.

2. In a medium bowl beat eggs and pour mixture over the tortilla layer. Cover with a lid and let cook over medium-low heat until firm. Add the salsa and the cheese. Re-cover with the lid and cook until the cheese is melted. Remove lid and arrange avocado slices over. Spoon onto plates and serve.

Dairy-Free Variation: *Omit cheese.*

Egg-Free Variation: *Use 1 cup (250 grams) silken tofu, scramble as directed. Or, use 1 cup chopped squash in place of eggs; sauté it with the onion.*

Good Morning Enchilada Strata
Serves 12

My husband loves when I make this dish. Conveniently, you can make it at night and cook it in the morning.

10 corn tortillas

1 cup (230 grams) sour cream

2 eggs

1 cup milk

1 cup (260 grams) salsa

1 15-ounce (420-gram) can black beans, drained

1½ cups (180 grams) jack cheese, divided

¼ cup (25 grams) spring onions, thinly sliced

1. Cut tortillas into strips. Set aside.
2. In a large bowl whisk together the sour cream, eggs, milk, and salsa.
3. In a greased 11-inch × 7-inch baking dish, layer the tortilla strips on the bottom. Sprinkle ⅓ of the beans and cheese over the tortillas. Save ½ cup of cheese. Repeat layers until all ingredients have been used. Pour the egg mixture over entire dish. Sprinkle with remaining cheese and spring onions. Cover and chill overnight.
4. Remove from refrigerator and bake in a 350°F (180°C) oven for 35 minutes. Cool slightly before serving.

Dairy-Free Variation: *Replace cheese with soy cheese or omit. Use 1 cup (250 grams) of pureed silken tofu for the sour cream. Omit milk and replace with soy or rice milk.*

Egg-Free Variation: *Omit eggs.*

ACCORDING TO Robert A. Wood, director of the Pediatric Allergy Clinic at Johns Hopkins in Baltimore, "recent studies indicate that growing up in a large family or a daycare center actually decreases the likelihood of developing an allergy. The fewer germs in terms of infection and the environment, the more time the immune system has to worry about things like allergens."

Scrambled Egg Enchiladas
Serves 6

Scrambled tofu is a good egg replacer for this. Just cut the recipe in half for a smaller family.

8 corn tortillas

1 tablespoon (15 grams) butter

¼ cup (35 grams) diced onion

¼ cup (30 grams) diced pepper

½ cup (55 grams) diced ham or cooked sausage pieces

8 eggs

1 cup (260 grams) mild enchilada sauce

½ cup (130 grams) salsa

1½ cups (180 grams) shredded cheese

2 tablespoons sliced spring onions

1. In a 350°F (180°C) oven, warm the tortillas.

2. Melt butter in a large frying pan over medium heat. Add onion and pepper, cook for 1 minute. Add the meat and cook 1 minute longer.

3. In a bowl beat eggs until frothy. Pour into frying pan and cook, stirring occasionally. Eggs should be set but not over-cooked or brown. Remove from heat and set aside.

4. Remove tortillas from the oven. Spoon ⅓ cup of the eggs down the center of the tortilla. Roll tortilla up and place seam-side down in an 11-inch × 7-inch baking dish. Set tortillas side-by-side.

5. Stir together the enchilada sauce and the salsa. Pour over tortillas. Top with cheese and spring onions. Return to the 350°F (180°C) oven and cook for 20 minutes. Serve immediately.

Dairy-Free Variation: Omit cheese; replace butter with margarine.

Egg-Free Variation: Replace eggs with 1½ cups (375 grams) silken tofu, crumbled.

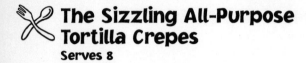

The Sizzling All-Purpose Tortilla Crepes
Serves 8

This is great for rolled meat and cheese, peanut butter and jam, and other cold fillings.

¼ cup (30 grams) cornstarch

½ cup (60 grams) rice flour

¼ cup tinned coconut milk

1 tablespoon oil

1 cup water

1. In a bowl whisk together cornstarch, rice flour, coconut milk, and water.

2. In a small frying pan or crepe pan, heat a little oil over medium-high heat. When very hot, pour about ⅔ cup of the mixture into the hot pan and swirl around to coat the bottom of the pan evenly. The mixture will bubble up all over, leaving holes covering the entire surface. When the sides of the crepe start to flip up, lift up with a spatula and check to see if the bottom is browned. Remove to a plate and cover. Repeat until all of the mixture has been used. Add a little more oil to the pan when needed.

3. The crepes will be very crunchy when first cooked. Fill with desired fillings and fold over. If using mayo, or jam, wrap with a paper towel because your crepe will be full of holes. Store covered in the refrigerator. They soften when they cool. I prefer to eat them hot. If these need to be reheated, do so in a frying pan; they crunch back up.

 # Fettuccine Alfredo
Serves 5

Rich and filling, this Alfredo is comforting on a cold night.

2 8-ounce (225-gram) boxes fettuccine or penne pasta

1 teaspoon or desired amount of fresh chopped garlic

¼ stick butter

1 16-ounce (455-gram) tub sour cream

1 cup (150 grams) Parmesan cheese, divided

¼ cup (15 grams) chopped fresh parsley

1. Cook noodles according to directions above, except keep noodles cold in the strainer.

2. In a large frying pan over medium heat, sauté the garlic in the butter. Add the tub of sour cream and stir until it is melted and has the consistency of cream. Add ½ cup (75 grams) Parmesan and turn the heat to low. Slowly add ¼ cup (40 grams) more of the Parmesan. Continue stirring until smooth.

3. Rinse noodles with warm water and place on a large plate. Pour the hot sauce over all the noodles. Sprinkle with remaining Parmesan and the fresh parsley.

Variation: Sauté shrimp in garlic and butter or cut strips of already baked chicken and sauté in garlic and butter. Place over noodles and sauce.

Dairy-Free Variation: Use sour cream substitute or plain soy or goat yogurt, soy Parmesan, and margarine.

Potato Noodles with Sour Cream Alfredo and Chives
Serves 8

Involve the whole family in this dish by letting the kids roll out the noodles.

Alfredo and Chives recipe (opposite page)

5 baking potatoes, scrubbed

½ cup (60 grams) potato flour, plus more for rolling

2 eggs

2 teaspoons salt

Dash pepper

1. Boil the whole potatoes in salted water until tender. Remove from water and let cool briefly.

2. Add all ingredients into a food processor and pulse until smooth. Turn dough out into a large bowl.

3. Keeping your hands well floured, scoop off a grape-sized portion of dough and roll into a 3-inch-long noodle. Place noodles on a lightly floured surface. Repeat until all the dough has been used.

4. Bring a large pot of water to a simmer. Roll the noodles into the water and cook for about 5 minutes. Remove with a slotted spoon. Place on a plate and set aside.

5. In a large oven-proof frying pan, sauté the noodles in olive oil over medium heat until the potato noodle is brown on both sides. Place in the oven at 300°F (150°C) and make the Alfredo with Chives. Pour Alfredo over warm noodles and serve.

6. If you want to freeze the noodles for later, omit stage 5. Cool noodles and place in a freezer bag. To defrost, bring to room temperature and then continue with stage 5.

Egg-Free Variation: Use 2 eggs' worth of Ener-G Egg Replacer and water.

ALTHOUGH COOKING for your child is the best way to go, sometimes it can't be avoided—you end up in a restaurant. Foods are not labeled in food-service operations, so you must ask the waiter, server, manager, or cook about ingredients. Unfortunately, cross-contamination can occur easily in a restaurant and accounts for some inadvertent food-allergy deaths.

Alfredo and Chives

Serves 8

2 teaspoons garlic, minced

¼ cup (60 grams) butter

2 cups (460 grams) sour cream

½ cup (75 grams) grated Parmesan

Dash nutmeg

½ cup (40 grams) chopped chives, spring onions, or parsley

1. In a frying pan over medium heat, sauté the garlic and the butter. Add the sour cream and Parmesan. Cook until bubbly. Remove from heat and stir in the nutmeg and the chives. Pour over noodles and serve.

Dairy-Free Variation: Use margarine and plain soy yogurt or mocha mix in place of sour cream. Omit Parmesan.

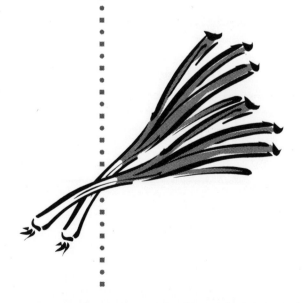

Pastitsio
Serves 8

Often called Greek lasagne, Pastitsio is a baked Greek casserole-like dish. If you opt for the lamb instead of minced beef, add ½ teaspoon cinnamon for a more ethnic flavor.

1 pound (455 grams) minced beef (or lamb for a more Greek flavor—see above)

½ cup (65 grams) onion, chopped

2 teaspoons garlic, minced

1 25-ounce (690-gram) jar pasta sauce

3 tablespoons (45 grams) butter

2 tablespoons cornstarch

1¾ cups milk

4 eggs

¾ cup (120 grams) grated Parmesan cheese, divided

1 13-ounce (370-gram) box elbow macaroni, cooked and drained

1. In a large frying pan cook meat, onion, and garlic until meat is brown. Drain fat. Stir in pasta sauce and simmer.

2. In a saucepan melt butter and cornstarch together. Add the milk and cook until thick and bubbly, about 3 minutes. Gradually stir in the beaten eggs. Add ½ cup of the Parmesan cheese. Stir until thick and then remove from heat. Pour 1 cup of mixture into a bowl and set aside.

GUESS WHO FOLLOWS a strict dairy- and wheat-free diet? Former Spice Girl Geri Halliwell, to name one person. Drew Barrymore is a vocal vegan along with the Material Girl, Madonna. Among celebrity circles, entertainers who claim to be allergic or intolerant to certain foods and cut out those foods from their diet entirely are called "Freebies," according to the July/August 2002 issue of *Health* magazine.

3. Pour the remaining sauce over the cooked noodles and mix until well coated.

4. In an 8-inch × 8-inch × 2-inch greased baking dish, layer half of the noodle mixture, all of the meat mixture, and the remaining noodle mixture. Pour the remaining 1 cup sauce over the top and sprinkle with the remaining cheese. Bake in a 350°F (180°C) oven for 40 minutes. Let stand 10 minutes before serving.

Variation: Sauté 2 cups (300 grams) of vegetables and use in place of the meat.

Dairy-Free Variation: Use equal amount of soy milk for the milk. Omit Parmesan.

Egg-Free Variation: Mix 4 eggs' worth of Ener-G Egg Replacer with water.

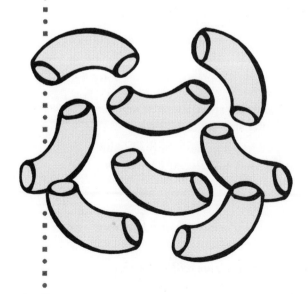

Risotto Parmesan Butternut Squash Bake
Serves 10

This wonderful food is great for anyone wanting to boost intake of resistance-building vitamins A and C.

4 cups water, divided

3 bouillon cubes

2 teaspoons oil

1 small courgette, shredded

2 cups (280 grams) peeled, cubed butternut squash

1 small onion, chopped

1½ cups (300 grams) arborio rice or short-grain brown rice

3 tablespoons (45 grams) butter

1 cup grated (150 grams) Parmesan cheese, divided

Salt and pepper

1. In a bowl, place 1 cup warm water and bouillon cubes; stir until dissolved.

2. In a medium saucepan over medium-high heat, add oil, courgette, squash, and onion. Cook for four minutes. Add rice and sauté for four minutes more. Add the 1 cup of bouillon liquid. Cook, stirring, until almost all liquid is absorbed. Add the remaining 3 cups of water. Cover saucepan and let cook until squash is tender and falling apart, about 25 minutes. Remove lid and stir in butter and half of the cheese.

3. Spoon mixture into a greased baking dish. Sprinkle with remaining cheese and bake in a 425°F (220°C) oven for 20 minutes. Cut into squares and serve.

Variation: When stirring in butter add 1 cup each fresh corn (160 grams) and chopped spinach (30 grams).

Dairy-Free Variation: Use soy Parmesan and margarine.

PARMESAN contains high-quality protein that's easily digested. Low in lactose, it is often suitable for people with lactose intolerance.

DO YOU KNOW the difference between a vegetarian and a vegan? Vegetarians eliminate all meat and fish from their diet. Vegans cut out all animal products entirely—including gelatin, eggs, and dairy along with meat and fish.

The Very Best Spaghetti
Serves 5

Rice noodles are delicate, but with the right attention they can be perfect. My advice for any gluten-free noodle is to cook it in a lot of water!

8 cups water
Salt and olive oil
2 8-ounce (225-gram) boxes of rice noodles
1 jar favorite spaghetti sauce
1 pound (455 grams) sautéed veggies and/or cooked meat
Parmesan for sprinkling (optional)

1. Bring 8 cups of water to a boil in a large pot. Add 1 teaspoon salt and a dash of oil.

   When water comes to a rolling boil, add the two boxes of noodles. With a wooden spoon, give the noodles a stir to prevent sticking. Turn down the heat to medium. Continue stirring, leaving pot uncovered. Every few minutes check a noodle to see the consistency. Often some noodles are crunchy while some are overcooked. This is why it is imperative to keep stirring the water and separating the noodles. When they are at a desired consistency, remove from heat and pour into a strainer. With a wooden spoon, gently stir and lift noodles while running them under cool water. After rinsing them they will feel firmer and less sticky. Shake strainer gently to discard any excess water. Place noodles on a large plate.

2. Bring your favorite spaghetti sauce with your choice of sautéed vegetables or meats to a complete boil. Pour over noodles, and try to coat all of the noodles with the sauce. You may keep the plate in a warm oven until ready to serve (no more than 20 minutes). Sprinkle with Parmesan.

Variation: For those little ones who prefer plain noodles, after rinsing with cool water, rinse with warm water. Heat butter or margarine in the microwave until melted and gently toss with noodles. Sprinkle with cheese or cooked veggies.

Inside Out Manicotti Pasta Bake
Serves 10

And yet another comfort food, perfect for a cold evening after playing during the day in a crisp park.

2 8-ounce (225-gram) boxes gluten-free noodle shapes

2 eggs

1 15-ounce (420-gram) container ricotta cheese

2 cups (240 grams) shredded mozzarella cheese, divided

½ cup (75 grams) grated Parmesan cheese, divided

¼ cup (15 grams) chopped parsley, divided

1 27-ounce (770-gram) jar marinara sauce

1. Cook noodles to package directions but remove them before they are too mushy; you want to keep them al dente. Rinse with cold water and set aside.

2. In a large bowl, stir together the eggs, ricotta, 1 cup of the mozzarella, half the Parmesan, and half of the parsley.

3. In a greased casserole dish, layer a bit of sauce, some noodles, and the cheese mixture. Repeat until all ingredients are gone. Sprinkle with the remaining cheese, Parmesan, and parsley. Bake in a 350°F (180°C) oven for 45 minutes. Let stand 5 minutes before serving.

Variation: *You may add a layer of sliced vegetables or cooked sausages if desired.*

Dairy-Free Variation: *Use 1 cup pureed silken tofu for ricotta. Omit other cheeses.*

Egg-Free Variation: *Omit eggs.*

TRY TO ALLEVIATE stress in your life and the lives of your children—especially your children allergic to foods. Researchers know that stress plays a major role in allergies by upsetting digestion, suppressing immunity, and weakening adrenal response.

Macaroni and Easy Cheese
Serves 4

What kid doesn't love macaroni and cheese?

1 8-ounce (225-gram) package elbow or spiral noodles

3 tablespoons (45 grams) butter

1 cheese packet from mac-n-cheese box (make sure packet is gluten-free)

2 teaspoons milk

1. Cook noodles according to package directions. Make sure to rinse well with cold water.

2. Put noodles in a clean saucepan. Stir in butter, cheese packet, and milk. On medium heat gently stir until all ingredients are thoroughly combined. Serve warm.

Variation: *Try adding cubed cooked hot dogs (or tofu dogs).*

Dairy-Free Variation: *Try the From-Scratch Mac-n-Cheese recipe (see page 108).*

From-Scratch Mac-n-Cheese
Serves 4

Serve this hearty Mac-n-Cheese with roasted chicken or chops.

4 teaspoons cornstarch

2 tablespoons (30 grams) butter

1 cup milk

½ cup (115 grams) sour cream

1 cup (120 grams) shredded cheddar

¼ cup (40 grams) grated Parmesan cheese

Salt and pepper

2 cups (280 grams) cooked, cooled elbow macaroni

1. In a large saucepan over medium heat add the cornstarch and butter. Stir until browned. Add the milk and bring to a boil until thickened. Stir in the sour cream and cheeses. Turn heat to low. Salt and pepper to taste. Add the macaroni and stir until heated thoroughly.

Variations: *For Confetti Macaroni, add 1 cup (125 grams) diced chicken, ham, or drained albacore. Use 1 cup (125 grams) assorted veggies like peas or broccoli. Stir until heated and cooked.*

Dairy-Free Variation: *Use 1 cup (250 grams) silken tofu or sour cream substitute, ½ cup soy milk, and ½ cup (60 grams) cheese alternative.*

PIZZAS

In a world where all the pizza is made with wheat flour, your family will love these alternative recipe pizza ideas that won't cause any allergic reactions.

 **Kids' Pizza-Pizza**
Serves 5

This is a kid-pleasing yeast- and gluten-free pizza. Make these in small springform pans and have your child create his or her own personalized pizza.

1½ cups (75 grams) instant mashed potatoes

1 cup milk

¼ cup butter, melted

2 teaspoons Italian seasonings

1 teaspoon garlic salt

¼ cup (40 grams) Parmesan

½ teaspoon sugar, optional

2 teaspoons oil

Optional sauce and toppings

1. In a food processor, combine all ingredients except for oil and optional sauce and toppings, and blend until well incorporated. Let dough sit for 10 minutes.

2. In a greased spring-form pan, push desired amount of dough on the bottom and halfway up the sides of the pan. You may have thin or thick dough.

3. Brush oil over dough and place in a 425°F (220°C) oven for about 30 minutes. Thinner dough might cook faster. If desired, turn the grill on and crisp the top for an additional 5 minutes. Remove and prepare your sauce and toppings.

Dairy-Free Variation: Use rice milk or water and margarine. Omit Parmesan.

Low-Sugar Variation: Omit sugar.

Homemade Pizza Dough
Makes one pizza

1½ cups warm water

2 tablespoons rapid rise yeast

7 teaspoons sugar

1 cup (125 grams) rice flour

1 cup (125 grams) masa corn flour

1 cup (50 grams) instant potato flakes or potato starch

2 teaspoons salt

2 tablespoons olive oil

1 teaspoon apple cider vinegar

3 teaspoons egg replacer

1. In a 2-cup measuring cup add water, yeast, and sugar. Let sit for 5 minutes.

2. In a mixer with paddle attachment add the flours, potato flakes, and salt. In a small bowl, cream together the oil, vinegar, and egg replacer. Pour the water and egg mixtures into the flour. Mix on low speed.

3. Remove from mixer, scrape dough off of paddle. Cover and let rise in a warm spot for 1 hour.

4. On a cornmeal-floured baking tray, or pizza pan, take desired amount of dough (2 cups for thin crust or 4 cups for thick crust). Push dough out into pan form. Spray dough and your hands with cooking spray if it gets too sticky. Brush with olive oil and sprinkle with garlic salt, if desired. Bake in a 400°F (200°C) oven for about 20 minutes. Remove and let cool. Add sauce, toppings, and cheese, bake for an additional 20 minutes.

5. Shape remaining dough into personal-size pizzas. Cook and freeze if needed.

Variation: Add 1 teaspoon rosemary, 2 tablespoons garlic, and ¼ cup (40 grams) grated Parmesan cheese to dough before baking. To make focaccia, add 1 4-ounce (115-gram) can tomato paste to dough with the added seasonings and cheese. Roll into a 2-inch thick rectangle and bake for about 35 minutes; sprinkle with cheese and bake another 15 minutes.

IF YOU'RE LOOKING for an in-depth gluten-free, allergy-free bread-baking book, try any by Bette Hagaman.

TO MAKE EASIER bread, use your favorite yeast bread mix (follow directions for loaf bread). Form into a pizza crust and brush with oil.

IF YOU HAVE KIDS who won't eat anything with onions in it, simply whirl all the ingredients in a food processor until smooth. Place in a sauce-pan and cook as directed.

MY OLDER CHILD enjoys the red sauce with mozzarella, pepperoni, and mushrooms. My little ones and I like the white sauce with cooked diced chicken, roma tomato slices, red peppers, mushrooms, spring onions, and cheddar cheese. The next time you pass a pizza restaurant, grab their menu, take it home, and have your kids "order" from you their favorite pizza toppings!

Red Sauce
Makes enough for one pizza

½ white onion, finely chopped, or 1 tablespoon dehydrated onion

1 tablespoon oil

1 6-ounce (170-gram) can Italian-style tomato paste

2 teaspoons sugar

1 teaspoon basil

1 teaspoon fresh, minced, or powdered garlic

Splash of gluten-free red wine

1. Sauté onion in oil. Add the can of tomato paste plus 1 can of water. Add the rest of the ingredients and stir until bubbly. Add more water if needed. Turn off heat and set aside.

Low-Sugar Variation: Omit sugar.

White Sauce
Makes enough for one pizza

1 cup (240 grams) ranch dressing

1 tablespoon fresh garlic, minced

½ cup (75 grams) grated Parmesan

1. In a small bowl, stir all ingredients together. Pour over pizza shell.

Dairy-Free Variation: Use soy ranch dressing, or use ¼ cup olive oil in place of the ranch. Use Parmesan substitute.

Vegetarian Potato Pizza
Serves 6

This can easily be turned into a vegan pizza by omitting the egg yolk.

3 medium baking potatoes, peeled

1 small onion

1 egg yolk

1 tablespoon potato flour or cornstarch

½ teaspoon salt

2 tablespoons olive oil

2 cups (250 grams) of your favorite sliced vegetables,
like courgette, mushrooms, onions, peppers,
and broccoli

2 teaspoons dried Italian seasonings

1 teaspoon chopped garlic

1 cup (120 grams) shredded mozzarella cheese

1. Shred potatoes and onion into a bowl of water; drain well,
   squeezing out excess moisture. In a large bowl combine
   potato and onion, egg yolk, flour, and salt. Mix well.

2. In a springform pan heat 2 teaspoons of oil in a 500°F
   (260°C) oven for 2 minutes. Remove from oven and press
   potato mixture into bottom of pan and up the sides. Brush
   the top with 2 teaspoons of oil. Return to the oven for about
   30 minutes until potato crust is brown and crisp.

3. In a large bowl, coat the 2 cups vegetables with the remaining
   oil, seasonings, and garlic. Top potato crust with cheese and
   spread the veggies on top.

4. Turn the oven down to 425°F (220°C) and return pizza
   to bake for 15 minutes or until veggies are cooked. Remove
   siding of the spring-form pan and serve.

Dairy-Free Variation: *Omit cheese.*

Egg-Free Variation: *Omit yolk and increase oil to 4 tablespoons.*

OILS ARE COMMONLY derived from allergenic foods like peanuts and soybeans. Caution must be exercised with oils in both choosing the "type" and the process of refinement. Generally, highly refined oils—even peanut oil—can be safe. Less highly refined oils, including cold-pressed oils, may not always prove safe. And always avoid using oils that have been used for frying. Cross-contamination can occur. Sesame seed oil used in Asian cooking is generally unrefined and not safe.

Upside-Down Pizza
Serves 6

Is it a casserole or a pizza? No matter—the taste buds love it!

1 pound (455-ounce) minced beef, turkey, or pork

½ cup (65 grams) each chopped onion and peppers

1 10-ounce (280-gram) jar spaghetti or pizza sauce

¼ cup (30 grams) pepperoni, chopped into small chunks

1 teaspoon Italian seasonings

¼ cup (40 grams) Parmesan cheese, divided

1 cup milk

1 cup (125 grams) rice or potato flour

2 teaspoons oil

2 eggs

2 cups (240 grams) shredded mozzarella or cheddar cheese

¼ cup (25 grams) chopped spring onions or olives

1. In a large frying pan cook minced meat with the onion and peppers. When meat is no longer pink in the center, add the sauce, pepperoni, seasonings, and half of the Parmesan. Simmer on medium heat until it bubbles; then remove from heat and set aside.

2. In a mixer add milk, flour, oil, and eggs. Beat at medium speed for 1 minute. Set aside.

3. In a greased spring-form pan, layer the meat mixture, shredded cheese, and then pour the egg mixture over the top. Sprinkle on the remaining Parmesan cheese and the spring onions or olives. Bake in a 425°F (220°C) oven for 30 minutes, or until firm and golden on the top. Remove and let sit for 5 minutes. Remove the sides of the spring-form pan and serve.

Dairy-Free Variation: Use cheese substitute.

Egg-Free Variation: Use 2 eggs' worth of Ener-G Replacer.

Polenta Crust Pizza
Serves 5

Just another variation of the wheat-crusted pizza. Polenta is made with cornmeal and adds a unique flavor. Bring on the pizza!

1 tube of premade polenta

1 sauce recipe

Favorite cheese and toppings

1. In a greased rectangular baking dish, slice or push polenta into the dish until it covers the entire surface. Pour the sauce over and top with cheese and toppings. Bake in a 350°F (180°C) oven for 45 minutes or until polenta is firm.

Dairy-Free Variation: *Omit cheese.*

BASICALLY, the ingredients statements on packaged foods are complete and accurate. This is especially important for consumers with allergies who need to avoid certain foods. Part of the task, however, is recognizing the terms on the ingredient statement or label that indicate the offending food. For example, for milk intolerances, look for caseinate, whey, and lactose. Want help identifying those items that you or your child needs to avoid because of a specific food allergy? Contact the Food Allergy and Anaphylaxis Network (www.foodallergy.org) for label-reading cards that can be used to teach you to recognize the terms to avoid.

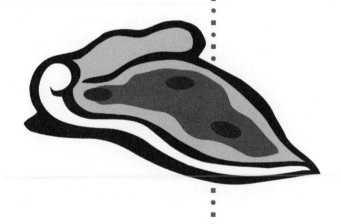

Pizza Stuffed Mushrooms
Serves about 6

All the great pizza flavor without any of the crust. Eating these treats is like popping pizza bites.

12 small portobello or 24 small white mushrooms

2 cups (240 grams) shredded mozzarella cheese, divided

½ cup (60 grams) coarsely chopped pepperoni

1 cup (260 grams) pizza sauce

½ cup (75 grams) grated Parmesan cheese, divided

1 courgette, diced

⅓ cup (40 grams) pepper, diced

¼ cup (35 grams) onion, chopped

1. Clean mushrooms, remove stems. On a lightly greased baking tray, place mushrooms open side up. Spray with cooking oil spray.

2. In a bowl mix together 1 cup (120 grams) of the mozzarella cheese, pepperoni, pizza sauce, half of the Parmesan cheese, courgette, pepper, and the onions. Spoon mixture into each mushroom. Sprinkle with remaining mozzarella and Parmesan cheeses. Bake in a 350°F (180°C) oven for 20 minutes. Remove and serve immediately.

Variation: You can stuff many different kinds of veggies. Cut a courgette in half lengthwise and hollow it out to stuff. Peppers also work nicely.

Dairy-Free Variation: Omit cheese.

 **Pizza Noodles**
Serves 6

Cheesy-saucy noodles make this a kid favorite.

2 8-ounce (225-gram) boxes of your favorite
    noodle shape

1 pound (455 grams) minced beef, pork, or turkey

1 10-ounce (280-gram) jar pizza or marinara sauce

⅓ cup (40 grams) chopped pepperoni

1 cup (70 grams) sliced mushrooms

2 tablespoons chopped olives

Splash of gluten-free red wine

2 cups (240 grams) shredded mozzarella cheese

Parmesan for sprinkling

2 tablespoons chopped fresh or dried parsley

1. Cook noodles according to package directions but remove
   them a few minutes before they are done; they should feel
   al dente. Rinse with cold water and set aside.

2. In a large frying pan, brown meat until no longer pink in the
   middle. Pour in sauce, pepperoni, mushrooms, and olives. Add
   a splash of wine if desired. Cook until bubbly. Turn off heat.

3. Scoop noodles into the sauce mixture and gently stir. Gently
   pour into a casserole dish. Top with cheeses and parsley. Bake
   in a 425°F (220°C) oven for about 15 minutes until cheese is
   melted and sauce is bubbly. Remove and serve.

*Variation: For Pizza Rice, replace the noodles with 2 cups
(330 grams) cooked rice. Add to sauce and bake as directed.*

Dairy-Free Variation: Omit cheese or use substitute.

*Gluten-Free Variation: Use gluten-free noodles in place of
regular noodles.*

THOUGH IT MAY prove difficult now to deal with your child's food allergies, take heart. Food allergies are frequently outgrown—especially milk, egg, and soybean allergies.

Tortilla Soup
Serves 8

A pleasing soup that can be made with or without chicken.

1 tablespoon olive oil

1 tablespoon corn flour (optional)

½ cup (65 grams) chopped onion

½ cup (60 grams) chopped green pepper

4 cups water

2 chicken or veggie bouillon cubes

1¾ cups (455 grams) chunky salsa

½ teaspoon ground cumin

1 15-ounce (420-gram) can black beans, drained

1 15-ounce (420-gram) can kidney or pinto beans, drained

2 cups (280 grams) cooked diced or shredded chicken

1 cup (160 grams) frozen corn

1 tablespoon oil

6 corn tortillas cut into ½-inch strips or tortilla chips

1. In a large pot, heat the oil and the corn flour until you have made a paste. Add the onions and peppers and cook for one minute. Add the water, bouillon cubes, salsa, cumin, beans, chicken, and corn. Bring to a boil and then turn heat to medium at a simmer. Cook covered for 10 minutes.

2. In a frying pan heat the oil and fry the tortilla pieces until crunchy, about 1 minute on each side. Sprinkle "chips" in soup or over individual bowls.

Harvest Soup
Serves 6

This is a wonderful winter soup. Omit the seasonings and you have the perfect baby food!

1 butternut squash

3 cups vegetable broth

1 large sweet potato

2 carrots

2 green apples

3 tablespoons (45 grams) butter

½ cup cream (optional)

½ teaspoon ginger

Salt and pepper

1. Peel and cube the butternut squash. Place squash and broth in a large stock pot. Bring to a boil and cook for 10 minutes. Lower heat to medium, and chop and add the sweet potato, carrots, and apples. Cook until tender, about 10 more minutes.

2. With a slotted spoon, scoop out the vegetables while tilting the spoon to drain the liquid, and place in a food processor or blender. Blend until all of the vegetables are smooth. Add broth if too thick.

3. Pour puree back into the chicken broth. Turn the heat up to medium high. Add the butter, cream, and ginger. Stir continually. When soup comes to a boil, turn heat to low. Add desired amounts of salt and pepper. Serve.

Variation: Use 3 chicken, beef, or veggie bouillon cubes and three cups of water in place of homemade broth.

Dairy-Free Variation: Omit cream and use margarine in place of butter.

FOR BABY FOOD, omit the broth, butter, ginger, cream, salt, and pepper. Let mixture cool in the refrigerator. Spoon into ice cube trays and wrap with tinfoil. Freeze. To defrost, place 1 cube into a saucepan and bring to room temperature over low heat. Test first before feeding to the baby.

Chicken Noodle Soup
Serves 8

Whereas we adults tend to love exotic flavors and a diversity of ingredients, kids' palates seem to prefer simpler tastes; this soup hits the mark.

2 teaspoons olive oil

1 cup (140 grams) cooked, cubed chicken

½ white onion, chopped

3 carrots, scrubbed and sliced

2 celery stalks, chopped

¼ teaspoon poultry seasoning

5 cups water

3 chicken bouillon cubes

1 cup (140 grams) cooked rice spaghetti, chilled

Salt and pepper

1. In a medium pot add oil, chicken, onion, carrots, and celery. Cook for 2 minutes on medium-high heat. Add the poultry seasoning.
2. Add the water and bouillon cubes; stir until dissolved. Cook uncovered for 15 minutes over medium heat.
3. Chop the spaghetti into 2-inch pieces. Add to soup and stir for 3 minutes. Add desired amounts of salt and pepper. Serve.

Mock Top Ramen Soup
Serves 5

Oh sure, you could go out and purchase ramen noodles—but the meal wouldn't be gluten-free. This noodle recipe mimics the most popular, packed ramen noodle meals on the market—without the possible allergens.

2 teaspoons sesame oil

2 carrots, scrubbed and diced small

¼ teaspoon ground ginger

1 cup (110 grams) tiny cooked shrimp or
    diced ham (optional)

5 cups water

3 bouillon cubes

2 tablespoons tamari

¼ cup (25 grams) spring onions, chopped

1 cup (130 grams) frozen peas

½ 15-ounce (420-gram) package gluten-free Asian thin noodles or spaghetti

1. In a medium pot add oil, carrots, ginger, and shrimp or ham. Cook for 1 minute.

2. Add the water and bouillon cubes; stir until dissolved. Add the tamari, spring onions, and peas.

3. In a separate pot bring 2 cups of water to a boil and add the Asian noodles. Let sit 2 minutes until soft. Rinse with cold water and chop into 8-inch-long pieces. Add to soup, stir, and serve.

Nut-Free Variation: *Use olive oil in place of sesame oil.*

ALLERGIES ARE GENETIC, making them much more likely to develop in children born to parents who suffer with either food or environmental allergies. The interesting part is this: The nature of the allergy that the child develops is not genetically controlled. For example, let's say that a child is born to parents who suffer from pollen allergies. One would think that the child will then develop pollen allergies, right? Perhaps, but the child may not develop pollen allergies at all but instead experience allergies to foods.

Grandma's Tamale Casserole
Serves 8

My grandma used to make this. When she gave me this recipe, I couldn't believe how easy it was to prepare.

1 pound (455 grams) minced beef or turkey

2 tablespoons oil

1 cup (130 grams) chopped onions

⅛ teaspoon garlic powder

1 teaspoon salt

2 teaspoon chili powder

2 8-ounce (225-gram) cans tomato sauce

1 15-ounce (420-gram) whole kernel corn, drained

½ cup (30 grams) parsley

1 15-ounce (420-gram) can pitted ripe olives, drained

1 beef bouillon cube

1 cup warm water

1 10½-ounce (295-gram) bag corn chips

2 cups (240 grams) Colby cheese, shredded

1. Brown beef in oil. Add the next nine ingredients. Place the bouillon cube in 1 cup of warm water and stir until dissolved. Stir into mixture, bring to a boil. Remove from heat and stir in the corn chips.

2. Pour mixture into a baking dish and top with cheese. Place in a 350°F (180°C) oven for 30 minutes. Let sit for 5 minutes before serving.

Dairy-Free Variation: Omit cheese.

Vegetarian Tamale Casserole
Serves 8

*I took my Grandma's recipe and lowered the fat. You still
get the same great taste and a little more color!*

1 14-ounce (395-gram) package corn tortillas

1 cup water

1 vegetable bouillon cube

2 8-ounce (225-gram) cans tomato paste

1 15-ounce (420-gram) can Mexican seasoned
   pinquito beans

½ cup (60 grams) each red and green bell
   peppers, chopped

1 cup (160 grams) frozen corn

2 teaspoons minced garlic

½ cup (30 grams) chopped coriander

¼ cup (30 grams) chopped olives

1 ripe tomato, chopped

1 courgette, chopped

2 tablespoons chopped green onion

2 teaspoons chili powder

1 cup (120 grams) shredded cheddar

1. Chop the corn tortillas into small pieces, set aside.

2. Heat 1 cup water in a saucepan. Add the bouillon cube; stir
   until dissolved. Add the tomato paste plus one can of water. Stir
   in the entire can of beans, peppers, corn, and garlic, half of the
   coriander, olives, tomato, courgette, green onion, and the chili
   powder. Add the chopped tortillas, reserving about ¼ cup.

3. Pour mixture into a baking dish. Top with remaining tortillas,
   cheese, and the remaining coriander. Bake in a 425°F (220°C)
   oven for 25 minutes. Let sit for 5 minutes and serve.

Dairy-Free Variation: *Omit cheese.*

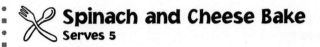

Spinach and Cheese Bake
Serves 5

A filling crustless quiche that the whole family loves.

5 eggs

1 cup (225 grams) cottage cheese

1 cup (120 grams) shredded jack cheese

½ teaspoon salt

Dash nutmeg

¼ cup (40 grams) Parmesan cheese

1 10-ounce (280-gram) package frozen chopped spinach, thawed and drained

1. In a large bowl, whisk together eggs, cottage cheese, ½ cup jack cheese, salt, nutmeg, and Parmesan. Stir in the spinach.

2. Pour into a greased 8-inch baking pan. Sprinkle with remaining cheese. Bake in a 350°F (180°C) oven for 30 minutes or until the middle is firm to the touch.

Variation: Add 1 cup (110 grams) cooked chopped shrimp, bacon, canned artichokes, or mushrooms after stirring in the spinach.

Dairy-Free Variation: Replace cottage cheese with 1 cup crumbled silken tofu; omit Parmesan and jack cheeses, or replace with dairy-free alternative.

Egg-Free Variation: Omit eggs and blend together ⅓ cup (40 grams) Ener-G Egg Replacer with 1 cup liquid. Add to step 1.

 **Chili-Mac**
Serves 5

Don't plan on serving leftovers for lunch the next day; there are never leftovers of this dish in my house.

1 box elbow macaroni

1 pound (455 grams) minced beef

¾ cup (95 grams) chopped onion

1 8-ounce (225-gram) can tomato paste

1 4-ounce (115-gram) can diced green
   chili peppers, drained

2 teaspoons chili powder

½ teaspoon salt

1 teaspoon minced garlic

1 15-ounce (420-gram) can red kidney
   beans, drained

½ cup (60 grams) shredded jack cheese

1. Cook noodles according to the package directions. Rinse with cold water and set aside.

2. In a frying pan, brown beef and onion until cooked completely. Stir in the tomato paste plus one can of water. Add the chili peppers, chili powder, salt, and garlic. Add the noodles and the kidney beans, stir. Top with cheese. Turn off heat and stir until cheese has melted. Serve.

Dairy-Free Variation: *Omit cheese.*

Gluten-Free Variation: *Use gluten-free macaroni in place of regular macaroni.*

 # Sloppy Joe Potato Skillet
Serves 5

1 pound (455 grams) minced beef or turkey

2 medium potatoes, chopped

1 onion, chopped

1 15½-ounce (430-gram) can Hunts Sloppy Joe sauce (gluten-free)

½ cup water

1. Brown meat, potatoes, and onion in a frying pan. Pour in the sauce and the water. Cover and simmer for 30 minutes or until potatoes are tender. Serve.

Upside-Down Shepherd's Pie
Serves 6

A meal in one dish—you get protein, dairy, and vegetables in this pie.

1⅓ cups (280 grams) instant mashed potatoes

2½ cups water, divided

2 tablespoons (30 grams) butter, divided

1 egg

1 teaspoon salt, divided

2 teaspoons dehydrated onions

2 chicken bouillon cubes

2 cups (460 grams) sour cream

1½ cups milk

½ teaspoon poultry seasoning

3 cups (420 grams) cubed cooked chicken or turkey

1 10-ounce (280-gram) package frozen mixed vegetables

1. To make potato crust, in a bowl combine the instant potatoes, 1 cup water, 1 teaspoon butter, egg, ½ teaspoon salt, and the dehydrated onions. Reserve ⅓ cup of the potato mixture. Push remaining mixture into a greased 10-inch springform pan or a 9-inch baking dish. Bake in a 400°F (200°C) oven for 10 minutes. Remove and set aside.

2. Mix bouillon cubes in remaining water until dissolved. In a large bowl combine the sour cream, milk, remaining butter and salt, poultry seasoning, bouillon water, and the reserved potato mixture. Stir in the chicken and veggies.

3. Pour into the potato crust. Bake in a 350°F (180°C) oven for 45 minutes.

4. You may reverse the recipe and put the chicken mixture on the bottom and layer the potato mixture on top.

Dairy-Free Variation: *Use soy yogurt in place of sour cream; use soy milk and margarine.*

Egg-Free Variation: *Omit egg.*

LACTOSE INTOLERANCE is a funny thing. Some people with lactose intolerance can actually tolerate milk products in small doses. It's up to each individual to determine how much is okay. While one person may be able to have a bowl of ice cream without any reaction, another may experience a problem while eating a food contaminated with dairy.

Wild Rice Bake
Serves 4

Another meal-in-one; it's also an excellent choice to make as a gift for a mother with a new baby, so she doesn't have to cook. Comforting and hearty, she and the new infant will thank you.

½ cup hot water

1 veggie bouillon cube

1 cup (230 grams) sour cream

2 teaspoons tamari

½ cup milk

2 cups (330 grams) cooked long grain wild rice

2 cups (280 grams) cubed cooked chicken, turkey, or ham

½ cup (35 grams) sliced mushrooms

½ cup (65 grams) frozen peas

½ cup (45 grams) broccoli florets

1. In a large bowl combine hot water and a bouillon cube; stir until dissolved. Whisk in the sour cream, tamari, and milk.

2. Stir in the rice, chicken, mushrooms, peas, and broccoli. Pour into a greased 2-quart casserole dish. Cover and bake at 350°F (180°C) for 45 minutes. Uncover and bake an additional 10 minutes. Let sit 10 minutes before serving.

Dairy-Free Variation: *Use soy milk and use soy yogurt in place of sour cream.*

 **Salmon Rice Pie**
Serves 6

Salmon is rich in the nutrients that make pretty skin.
The fish has actually been touted as an anti-aging food.
Add a salad to this main dish for a light summer dinner.

1½ cups (250 grams) cooked white rice

4 eggs, divided

1½ cups (180 grams) crumbled feta cheese, divided
(optional)

1 cup milk

1 tablespoon potato flour or cornstarch

1 cup (225 grams) cooked boneless salmon fillet,
    coarsely chopped

1 cup (30 grams) chopped fresh spinach

1 teaspoon minced garlic

½ teaspoon salt

¼ cup (25 grams) sliced spring onions

1. Grease a 9-inch glass pie plate. In a small bowl mix together
   rice, 1 egg, and 1 cup of the feta cheese. Push rice up the
   sides and bottom of the pie plate. Wet your hands if rice is
   sticky. Place in a 325°F (170°C) oven for 15 minutes. Remove
   from oven and set aside.

2. In a bowl stir milk, flour, and 3 eggs. Add the salmon,
   chopped spinach, ½ cup (60 grams) feta cheese, garlic, salt,
   and spring onions. Pour into the pie dish. Bake for 45 minutes or until a knife in the center comes out clean. Remove
   and let sit 10 minutes before serving.

Dairy-Free Variation: Omit feta cheese and use soy milk.

*Egg-Free Variation: Use 1 egg worth of Ener-G Egg Replacer in
crust and 3 eggs' worth in filling.*

Layered Vegetarian Enchiladas
Serves 8

This is such a beautiful dish. You can see all of the colorful layers. Make sure to bring this to any potluck you attend.

1 cup (120 grams) each chopped courgette, red pepper, and red onion

1 teaspoon oil

1 8-ounce (225-gram) tub ricotta cheese

¼ cup (40 grams) grated Parmesan cheese

2 eggs

2 cups (240 grams) shredded Colby cheese, divided

1 4-ounce (115-gram) can diced green chilies, undrained

12 8-inch corn tortillas

1 15-ounce (420-gram) can refried beans

1½ cups (390 grams) mild green or red enchilada sauce

¼ cup (25 grams) chopped spring onions

1. In a frying pan cook the courgette, red pepper, and onion in oil for 3 minutes.

2. In a bowl whisk together the ricotta cheese, Parmesan cheese, eggs, ½ cup of Colby cheese, and the can of chilies.

3. In a greased springform pan layer tortillas on bottom, covering surface completely. Spread the refried beans over surface. Sprinkle with ¼ cup Colby cheese. Layer with more tortillas. Pour the vegetables over. Add more tortillas. Spread the ricotta cheese mixture over. Add the remaining tortillas. Pour sauce over. Sprinkle with remaining cheese and spring onions.

4. Let sit for 1 hour to 24 hours, covered, in the refrigerator.

5. Bake in a 375°F (190°C) degree oven for 40 minutes. Let cool 10 minutes. Remove rim from pan. Serve.

Dairy-Free Variation: Omit cheeses. Replace with an additional layer of veggies or beans and additional sauce.

Egg-Free Variation: Omit eggs.

Broccoli Beef Noodles
Serves 6

4 teaspoons sesame oil

1 cup (175 grams) sliced fajita meat

2 teaspoons molasses

2 tablespoons tamari

2 teaspoons grated gingerroot

1 beef bouillon cube

1 tablespoon cornstarch

1 cup warm water

1 cup (90 grams) sliced broccoli

2 cups (280 grams) cooked gluten-free spaghetti noodles

¼ cup (25 grams) sliced spring onions

1. In a frying pan over medium-high heat, add 2 teaspoons sesame oil and the meat. Sauté until fully cooked. Add the molasses, tamari, and ginger. Coat the meat. Add the beef cube and cornstarch to the water and stir until dissolved. Add the broccoli to the steak and stir to coat. Add the water mixture. Let cook until thickened.

2. Add the noodles, spring onions, and 2 teaspoons of sesame oil. Cook until heated. Serve.

Low-Sugar Variation: Replace molasses with Whey Low.
Nut-Free Variation: Replace sesame oil with olive oil.

GINGER MAY contain negligible nutrients but is invaluable as a flavor enhancer. Add fresh ginger to your meats and vegetables for a little pizzazz. Interestingly, ginger also seems to relieve motion sickness and can alleviate morning sickness associated with pregnancy. As little as 1 gram can reduce motion-induced nausea and vomiting, according to one scientific study. Just to let you know, powdered ginger is spicy with a slightly musty flavor, but fresh root ginger is sweet and tangy. So choose the ginger that best suits your taste buds.

ACCORDING TO the Food Allergy and Anaphylaxis Network (FAAN), severe food allergy reactions account for an estimated 30,000 emergency room visits, 2,000 hospitalizations, and 200 deaths each year.

Fishy Sticks
Serves 6

2 eggs

¼ cup milk

1 cup (115 grams) gluten-free crouton or cracker crumbs

1 cup (125 grams) rice flour

1 pound (455 grams) cod fillets, cut into ½-inch strips

⅓ cup oil

1. In a small bowl whisk together eggs and milk.

2. In a food processor or blender pulse the croutons and the flour until you get smooth flour. Pour onto a plate.

3. Rinse and pat the fish dry with paper towels. Dip each piece of fish into egg mixture, and then roll in the flour mixture.

4. Add the oil to a hot frying pan over medium-high heat. Cook until golden on the outside and white in the center. Place on a paper towel-lined plate. Serve with Tartar Sauce (below).

Dairy-Free Variation: Use water in place of milk.

Egg-Free Variation: Cream together 2 teaspoons Ener-G Egg Replacer with 2 tablespoons water.

Tartar Sauce
Makes about 1 cup (235 grams)

1 cup (235 grams) mayonnaise

1 teaspoon mustard

1 tablespoon minced spring onions

¼ cup (60 grams) dill or sweet pickles, minced

1 teaspoon Tabasco sauce

1. Mix all ingredients well. Serve with fish sticks.

Egg-Free Variation: Use egg-free mayo.

Chicken Nuggets with Sweet Dipping Sauce
Serves 10

My husband invented these for us! So simple and delicious, you will never miss your nuggets again! You can even freeze these for a quick lunch—just like the real deal but healthier and better tasting.

1 pound (455 grams) chicken breast, cut into chunks

1 egg

2 tablespoons oil

2 teaspoons each tamari and oil

1 teaspoon each salt and sugar

½ teaspoon poultry seasoning

¼ teaspoon each black pepper and garlic powder

¼ cup water

½ cup (60 grams) rice flour

¼ cup (30 grams) corn or rice starch

½ teaspoon baking soda

1. Wash cut chicken in cold water. Mix together egg, oil, tamari, salt, sugar, poultry seasonings, pepper, and garlic powder in a large plastic freezer bag. Place chicken into bag and shake, coating each piece.

2. Place bag into freezer for about 30 minutes. Remove from freezer and pour the water into the bag; shake again.

3. In a bowl, mix the flour, cornstarch, and baking soda. Pour into the bag with the chicken. Shake again to coat.

ONE WAY food allergy specialists say you can avoid your child's susceptibility to food allergies is to begin while you're pregnant. Women should avoid peanuts, tree nuts, and shellfish while pregnant and also while breastfeeding. Then avoid giving a baby cow's milk or other diary products until the child's first birthday. Don't introduce eggs until eighteen to twenty-four months. Finally, to safeguard against the child's having a reaction to peanuts, wait until a child is three to give them to him or her.

4. In a hot frying pan with 1 inch of oil, place a few nuggets at a time and fry until golden brown on both sides, about 3 minutes per side. Remove to a plate lined with paper towels to drain. Repeat with remaining nuggets. Serve with Sweet Dipping Sauce.

5. To store, let nuggets cool to room temperature. Place in a heavy-duty plastic freezer bag. Try to press as much air as possible out of the bag before placing in the freezer. Can be kept frozen up to 3 weeks. To heat frozen nuggets, place in a 350°F (180°C) oven for 10 minutes, or microwave.

Egg-Free Variation: Use 2 eggs' worth of Ener-G Egg Replacer.

 ## Sweet Dipping Sauce
Makes 1 cup (300 grams)

½ cup (125 grams) Dijon or honey mustard

3 tablespoons rice vinegar

¼ cup olive oil

½ cup (170 grams) honey

1 tablespoon brown sugar (optional)

1. Whisk all ingredients in a bowl. Serve with nuggets. Refrigerate leftovers, covered, for 4 days.

Low-Sugar Variation: Omit honey and sugar and replace with ½ cup Whey Low.

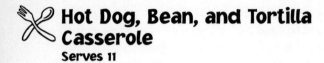

Hot Dog, Bean, and Tortilla Casserole
Serves 11

A variation on the old standby "beanies and weenies" that kids just love.

11 corn tortillas

11 chicken hot dogs

1 15-ounce (420-gram) can Mexican seasoned beans or barbequed beans

2 cups (520 grams) purchased salsa

1 cup (120 grams) shredded Colby cheese

1. Take a few tortillas at a time, sprinkle them with water, and microwave for about 30 seconds until soft. Repeat with remaining tortillas. Set aside, covered.

2. In each tortilla place 1 hot dog and add 3 tablespoons beans. Roll up and place seam-side down next to each other in a greased 13-inch × 9-inch pan. Pour salsa over entire dish. Sprinkle with cheese. Bake in a 350°F (180°C) oven for 20 minutes.

Dairy-Free Variation: *Omit cheese.*

Hebrew National hot dogs are gluten-free and, therefore, a great choice to use in any recipes calling for hot dogs. Read the label on meatless hot dogs; it is hard to find a brand without gluten.

Corn Dogs
Serves 10

I make these without the sticks—they are just as good as the store-bought ones.

10 hot dogs
1 cup (125 grams) masa corn flour
½ cup (70 grams) cornmeal
⅓ cup (115 grams) honey or (40 grams) sugar
1 egg
1½ teaspoons baking powder
½ teaspoon dry mustard
1 cup milk or water
½ cup olive oil, divided

1. Rinse hot dogs with water and pat dry.
2. In a medium-size bowl mix together the masa flour, cornmeal, honey, egg, baking powder, dry mustard, milk, and 2 tablespoons oil.
3. Heat the remaining oil in a frying pan until hot. Dip a hot dog into the batter and coat well. Shake off excess. Fry two at a time. Cook until golden. Remove to a paper towel-lined plate and drain. Serve with favorite hot dog dips.
4. To freeze, let come to room temperature. Wrap in foil or wax paper and place in a heavy-duty freezer bag. Freeze for up to 1 month.

Variation: For mini corn dogs, cut each hot dog into 3 pieces. Coat with batter and fry until golden.

Egg-Free Variation: Use 1 egg's worth of Ener-G Egg Replacer.

Low-Sugar Variation: Replace sugar with Whey Low.

Taco Salad Meal
Serves about 8

Double this recipe for a large crowd. You will be surprised at how filling this salad is. I like this salad with both the salsa vinaigrette and the ranch dressing.

½ pound (225 grams) minced beef

1 teaspoon garlic powder

1 teaspoon onion salt

1 tablespoon chili powder

1 head romaine lettuce

1 15-ounce (420-gram) can kidney beans, drained

1 15-ounce (420-gram) can black beans, drained

½ cup (60 grams) shredded jicama

1 medium cucumber, sliced

¼ cup (15 grams) chopped coriander

¼ cup (25 grams) sliced spring onions

1 avocado, sliced

1 firm tomato, chopped

1 cup (120 grams) shredded cheese (optional)

1 cup (115 grams) crushed tortilla chips

1 recipe Ranch Dressing, Salsa Vinaigrette, or
   Honey Mustard

1. In a frying pan brown the beef over medium heat. Add the garlic powder, onion salt, and chili powder. Cook until no longer pink. Drain fat; set aside to cool.

2. Clean and chop the lettuce and place in a large bowl. Add the beans, jicama, cucumber, coriander, spring onions, avocado, and tomato. Sprinkle with meat, cheese, and the tortilla chips. Serve with desired dressing on the side or over the top.

Dairy-Free Variation: Omit cheese.

136

ONCE A FOOD ALLERGY has been diagnosed, there are several key things that you should do to avoid your child's suffering in the future. They are:

• Read labels—make sure you avoid all products with the allergen.

• Prepare for an emergency—have antihistamines or Epipen on hand in case your child mistakenly eats an allergic food.

• Tell everyone—the sitter, Grandma and Grandpa, playmates' parents; explain that your child must eat only food given by you or approved by you.

Ranch Dressing
Makes about 1 cup (240 grams)

½ cup buttermilk
½ cup (115 grams) sour cream
1 tablespoon minced onion
2 tablespoons minced chives or spring onions
1 teaspoon garlic powder
1 tablespoon chopped parsley
¼ teaspoon each salt and pepper
Squeeze of lemon juice

1. Whisk all ingredients in a bowl. Chill until ready to serve. Use within 1 week.

Dairy-Free Variation: Replace ½ cup buttermilk with ¼ cup soy yogurt, ¼ cup rice milk, and ½ Tablespoon lemon juice. Replace sour cream with soy yogurt.

Salsa Vinaigrette
Makes about 1 cup (235 grams)

½ cup (130 grams) purchased salsa

¼ cup olive oil

¼ cup rice vinegar

1. Whisk all ingredients together and serve. Store for 1 week in the refrigerator.

Honey Mustard
Makes 1 cup (235 grams)

¼ cup olive oil

¼ cup rice vinegar

3 basil leaves, cleaned

1 tablespoon Dijon mustard

1 tablespoon honey

Dash gluten-free wine

Salt and pepper

1. Place all ingredients in a food processor. Pulse until smooth. Serve immediately.

Low-Sugar Variation: *Replace honey with 1 tablespoon Whey Low.*

WE KNOW THAT you read labels. You have to, for goodness sake! But if a label refers to "flavoring" or "spices" without designating exactly what they are, pass it up. Sounds cliché, but it's better to be safe than sorry.

138

MCDONALD'S DOES a great job of displaying for consumers the allergens in the food on their menu. You will be happy to see what you are able to eat at this fast food giant. Just navigate online to their Web site at www.mcdonalds.com for a list.

Happy Burgers
Serves 6

Whenever your child wants a fast food burger meal, make this burger, wrap it in wax paper, and serve it with frozen gluten-free French fries and soda or a frozen yogurt milkshake! I have even gone as far as purchasing the toy and a soda from a fast food restaurant and serving them along with this meal in the restaurant's kid's meals bag (ask for the toy to be inside a meal bag).

1 pound (455 grams) minced beef or turkey

1 teaspoon Worcestershire sauce

½ teaspoon each garlic and onion powder

Salt and pepper

½ cup (120 grams) mayonnaise

¼ cup (60 grams) catsup

1 teaspoon mustard

2 teaspoons sweet or dill relish

5–6 whole lettuce leaves, washed and dried
 (I prefer iceberg)

5–6 slices American cheese

1. In a medium bowl mash together first 4 ingredients with a fork. Form patties and fry in a frying pan until no longer pink in the middle.

2. In a small bowl mix together the mayonnaise, catsup, mustard, and relish.

3. Place a piece of wax paper on a flat surface. Put a piece of lettuce with the curved side up, like a bowl, on the paper. Place a hot beef patty in the center. Add cheese. Spoon on desired amount of sauce. Fold 2 opposite sides of the lettuce over the meat. Fold next 2 sides over. Wrap in wax paper. Serve as directed above.

Dairy-Free Variation: *Omit cheese.*

Egg-Free Variation: *Use egg-free mayo.*

SIDE DISHES

Most every main dish requires a side dish—a salad, a potato, a bread, a veggie! You wouldn't think about serving your child a slab of meat and nothing more. Parents want to ensure their children eat balanced meals. These recipes offer tasty and healthy ways to fill out your child's plate and help him/her fill up on nurtition without suffering any illness. From cornbread to chili bean bake and back, your child will clean his/her whole plate.

Curried Rice
Serves 5

My children do not usually enjoy spicy things, but they do like this mildly spicy, sweet rice dish. Add a fruit salad and some baked fish or chicken on the side to make a nice meal.

1 tablespoon olive oil

¼ cup (35 grams) chopped white onion

½ cup (60 grams) chopped celery

1 cup (130 grams) chopped carrots

⅔ cup (110 grams) long-grain white rice

1 vegetable bouillon cube plus 1¼ cups water

1 teaspoon curry powder

⅓ cup (50 grams) currants

¼ cup (15 grams) chopped fresh parsley

¼ cup (30 grams) chopped roasted nuts—almonds, peanuts, or pecans (optional)

1. In frying pan heat oil with the onion, celery, and the carrots. Add the rice and cook for a minute, or until rice starts to change color. Pour in the bouillon cube mixed with the water. Add the curry powder and the currants; cover and cook over medium-low heat for about 25–30 minutes or until rice is tender. Stir in the parsley and the nuts. Serve.

Nut-Free Variation: Omit nuts.

ALTHOUGH anaphylaxis requires immediate attention and a call to 911, most symptoms associated with an allergy can be eased right away with an anti-allergy medication that contains diphenhydramine. These antihistamines block histamines, the chemicals that cause allergic symptoms. Check with your doctor about which medication to have on hand if you have a child with a food allergy.

Teriyaki Veggie Spears
Makes 2 cups (300 grams)

Steamed or baked vegetables can be downright bland. By glazing them with this great teriyaki sauce, the flave-ometer goes way up and little ones eat all their veggies. Thank you, Lori, for this great idea!

1 pound (455 grams) fresh vegetables (asparagus, carrots, broccoli, or mushrooms)

⅓ cup gluten-free tamari

1 tablespoon sesame oil

¼ cup (85 grams) honey

¼ cup (30 grams) sesame seeds

1. Clean and cut the vegetables into long spears. Place on an oil-sprayed broiling pan. Mix the tamari, oil, and the honey. Drizzle over the veggies. Sprinkle with the sesame seeds. Bake in a 425°F (220°C) oven for about 10 minutes. Remove and cool before serving. They are tasty cold, too!

Low-Sugar Variation: *Replace honey with Whey Low.*

Nut-Free Variation: *Omit sesame seeds and replace sesame oil with olive oil.*

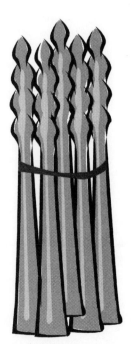

Whipped Sweet Potatoes
Serves 6

My family thinks this dish tastes better with gravy than regular mashed potatoes, so be warned: You may replace your old holiday russet potatoes with this delicious dish.

5 medium sweet potatoes (or yams, if you prefer)

⅔ cup milk

¼ stick butter

1 bouillon cube

Salt and pepper to taste

1. Scrub the potatoes and wrap in tinfoil. Bake in a 400°F (200°C) oven for about an hour or until soft. Cool and peel. Cut off ends and place in a mixer.

2. Heat the milk, butter, and bouillon cube in a microwave. Add to potatoes and whip on medium speed until smooth. You may add more milk to achieve desired consistency. Add salt and pepper to taste.

Dairy-Free Variation: *Replace milk with water and butter with margarine.*

THANKFULLY, today many places recognize the need for gluten-free products. Contact these companies that specialize in gluten-free products:

Cecilia's Gluten-Free Grocery

(800) 491-2760

www.glutenfreegrocery.com

Gluten Solutions

(888)845-8836

www.glutensolutions.com

Gluten Free Mall (online only)

www.glutenfreemall.com

IF YOU OR YOUR CHILD has been suffering with celiac disease for a long time and only recently realized what the problem was, take heart. If you swear off gluten, most of the symptoms and problems associated with celiac disease disappear within six months.

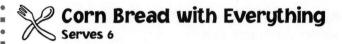

Corn Bread with Everything
Serves 6

This complements any home-style meal.

¼ cup (60 grams) butter, room temperature

¼ cup (50 grams) sugar

3 eggs

1 cup (125 grams) masa corn flour

⅔ cup (100 grams) cornmeal

2 teaspoons baking powder

1 teaspoon baking soda

½ teaspoon salt

1¼ cups (290 grams) sour cream

½ cup (50 grams) sliced spring onions

1 cup (160 grams) frozen corn

1½ cups (180 grams) shredded cheese

1. In a mixer cream together the butter and the sugar. Add the eggs and blend. Add the flour, cornmeal, baking powder and soda, salt, and sour cream. Blend until smooth. By hand, stir in the spring onions, corn, and shredded cheese.

2. Pour into a greased 9-inch baking pan or quiche pan. Bake in a 350°F (180°C) oven for 25 minutes.

Variation: Add 1 cup (120 grams) chopped green chilies or ½ cup (60 grams) sliced mild jalapenos to the batter.

Dairy-Free Variation: Use margarine or olive oil in place of butter. Use equal amounts of plain soy yogurt or 1 cup (250 grams) silken tofu in place of sour cream. Replace cheese with dairy-free alternative, or omit.

Egg-Free Variation: Omit eggs, add ⅓ cup oil.

Mexican-Style Baked Beans
Serves 8 as a side dish

Just a little variation on the old American favorite!

1 teaspoon oil

½ cup (65 grams) chopped onions

¼ cup (60 grams) brown sugar

1 15-ounce (420-gram) can Mexican seasoned
   pinquito beans

1 15-ounce (420-gram) can pinto, black, or
   navy beans, drained

1 cup (250 grams) barbecue sauce

½ cup (120 grams) catsup

3 tablespoons molasses

¼ cup (15 grams) coriander

Salt and pepper

1. In a pot combine oil, onions, and brown sugar. Cook for
   1 minute. Add the cans of beans, barbecue sauce, catsup, and
   molasses. Cook on medium heat until mixture begins to boil.
   Turn heat to low, add the coriander. Stir in the salt and pepper to taste. Cook on low for 30 minutes, covered. Let sit
   10 minutes before serving.

Low-Sugar Variation: *Omit sugar and molasses. Use 1 cup
sugar-free catsup in place of regular catsup.*

ACCORDING TO *Prevention* magazine's November 1, 2000, issue (Volume 52,
Issue 11), it takes an average of ten years
and just as many different physicians to
be diagnosed with celiac disease.

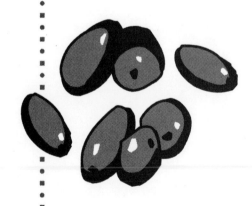

SOYBEANS ARE USED in everything from ink to baby formula, but many people are allergic to the bean (specifically, a protein within the bean's make-up). Scientists, however, have found out how to "shut off" the gene that makes the allergenic protein in the crop's seed. According to *Agricultural Research* (September 2002), plant physiologists have knocked out this dominant human allergen using biotechnology. Soybeans, along with eggs, milk, peanuts, wheat, fish, shellfish, and tree nuts are considered one of the "big eight" food allergens.

Red Potatoes
Serves 8

These are my favorite seasoned potatoes and are especially good with Happy Burgers. Once again, this is my husband's creation!

8 red potatoes, scrubbed and cut into wedges
3 tablespoons olive oil
1½ teaspoons pepper
¼ teaspoon salt
½ teaspoon garlic powder
2 tablespoons paprika
1 teaspoon chili powder

1. In a large pot bring 8 cups of salted water to a boil. Place the potatoes in the pot and boil for 2 minutes until barely soft (you want them to be firm, not mushy). Strain and place in a large bowl and toss with oil.

2. Add seasonings and stir to coat.

3. Place on a greased cookie sheet and bake in a 400°F (200°C) oven for 20 minutes, or until golden and crisp. Serve.

Green Bean Bake
Serves 6

This is a family-pleasing side dish and complements any main coarse.

½ cup (60 grams) rice flour

½ teaspoon each garlic salt and pepper

2 tablespoons oil

½ white onion, sliced

1 cup (230 grams) sour cream

½ cup milk

2 tablespoons tamari

4 cups (500 grams) fresh or frozen green beans, cut

1 cup (70 grams) sliced mushrooms

1. In a bowl combine flour, garlic salt, and pepper. Heat a frying pan with oil until hot. Toss the onion slices in the flour and place in the hot frying pan. Fry until golden, 2 minutes.
2. In a large bowl mix the sour cream, milk, and tamari. Stir in the beans and mushrooms.
3. Pour into a 9-inch baking pan. Top with onions. Bake for 30 minutes in a 350°F (180°C) oven.

Dairy-Free Variation: Omit sour cream and milk. Use 1½ cups (375 grams) of Imagine's dairy-free mushroom soup.

ACCORDING TO the January 15, 2003, edition of *The Independent* (London, England), before 1950, an allergy to cow's milk was considered very rare. But now, a French research team found evidence to suspect that milk allergies affect 10 percent of infants and 5 percent of older children.

THE FOOD ALLERGY and Ana-phylaxis Network (FAAN) is an organization that alerts the public about foods that may be mislabeled or cross-contaminated during manufacture and production. Founded in 1991, FAAN supports research and public awareness of food allergies and anaphylaxis. Find information on the organization's Web site at www.foodallergy.org.

Green Chile Bean Bake
Serves 6

Whenever I make food with a "Mexican" theme, I make sure to include this side dish.

1 15½-ounce (430-gram) can refried beans

4 tablespoons corn flour

1 cup milk

1 cup (230 grams) sour cream

1 7-ounce (200-gram) can diced green chilies

4 eggs

1 cup (120 grams) shredded jack or cheddar cheese, divided

1 cup (260 grams) salsa (optional)

1. Spread the refried beans in a 9-inch greased baking pan.

2. In a bowl whisk together the flour, milk, sour cream, undrained chilies, and eggs. Pour over the beans. Sprinkle with ½ cup (60 grams) of cheese, pour the salsa over, and sprinkle with remaining cheese. Bake in a 350°F (180°C) oven for 30 minutes. Let stand 10 minutes before serving.

Dairy-Free Variation: Use 1 cup silken tofu (250 grams) and 1 cup soy milk to replace the milk, sour cream, and cheese.

Egg-Free Variation: Omit eggs; use 4 teaspoons Ener-G Egg Replacer and 4 tablespoons water. Cream together and add to milk mixture.

Cheesy Little Corn Cakes
Serves 5

On a warm day, these go great with a crisp salad.

¾ cup (90 grams) masa corn flour

⅓ cup (40 grams) shredded cheese

3 tablespoons butter, melted

½ teaspoon salt

¾ cup boiling water

⅔ cup (100 grams) frozen corn

1. In a bowl mix together the flour, cheese, butter, and salt.
   Slowly add the boiling water. Stir to make a thick batter.
   Stir in the corn.

2. Heat a large nonstick frying pan over medium-high heat. You
   may add oil to the pan if needed. Add a quarter-size amount
   of batter to the frying pan and cook until brown on each side.
   Serve warm as an accompaniment to any meal.

   If needed, make the whole batch, bring to room temperature,
   and freeze in a zipper-lock bag. Reheat in a 350°F (180°C)
   oven for about 10 minutes.

Dairy-Free Variation: *Use dairy-free cheese substitute, or omit.
Use margarine in place of butter.*

THINK ABOUT ALL the foods that don't contain gluten: all fruits, all vegetables, rice, corn, nuts, potatoes, red meat, chicken, fish, eggs, and dairy products. There really is a world of food out there to feed your wee ones.

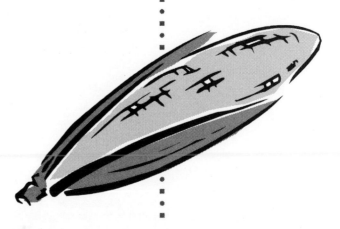

 **Fried Rice**
Serves 5

Have a theme dinner night and include this side dish with Teriyaki Veggie Spears, and use the same sauce for your cooked chicken strips.

2 tablespoons sesame oil, divided

2 eggs, beaten

1 teaspoon ground ginger

2 carrots, scrubbed and sliced

½ cup (55 grams) cubed cooked ham (optional)

3 cups (500 grams) leftover plain rice, cooked

¼ cup (25 grams) sliced spring onions

2 tablespoons tamari

1 cup (130 grams) frozen peas

1. In a crepe pan or small frying pan heat 1 tablespoon oil until hot. Add the beaten eggs and whirl in pan to spread evenly, like a crepe. Cook without stirring until set. Slide onto a cutting board and slice up into short narrow strips.

2. In a large frying pan, add remaining oil, ginger, carrot, and ham. Cook for 1 minute. Add the rice, green onion, tamari, and peas. Stir. Cover and let cook for 6 minutes. Stir in the egg and add additional tamari if desired.

Egg-Free Variation: *Omit eggs.*

Nut-Free Variation: *Replace sesame oil with olive oil.*

 **Sweet Potato Hash**
Serves 5

Try this in place of hash browns.

1 large sweet potato, scrubbed and grated
¼ cup (35 grams) grated onion
1 egg
2 tablespoons chopped coriander
¼ cup (25 grams) rice bran or rice flour
½ teaspoon salt
2 teaspoons olive oil

1. In a large bowl, mix together all ingredients.

2. In a large greased frying pan over medium-high heat, add potato mixture and flatten across pan. Cover and cook for 10 minutes. With a spatula, flip sections over and cook an additional 5 minutes. Serve.

3. For pancakes, form patties and fry a few at a time, 5 minutes on each side.

Egg-Free Variation: Use 1 egg worth of Ener-G Egg Replacer.

OLIVE OIL is perfect for today's healthy lifestyle because it has no cholesterol and is one of the oils highest in monounsaturated fats. For people who must avoid hydrogenated oil, olive oil is an acceptable choice for cooking, frying, and replacing butter and oil in baked goods.

SWEETS AND TREATS

Gooey desserts, tasty candies, and yummy creations—every kid loves sweets! And every child deserves a little taste-bud-fun occasionally. This section caters to a child's sweet tooth. So many parents with little ones suffering from food allergies can't find yummy treats that won't make their children sick. These recipes will put a smile and an icing smear on any child's face and won't make a wee one with food allergies ill. So go ahead, pass out the cookies, cakes and pies.

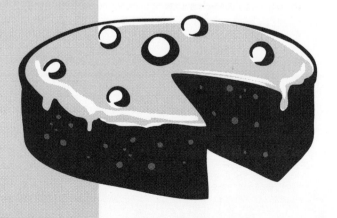

Vanilla Chip Cookies
Makes about 36

Nobody ever believes that this awesome cookie is made with only rice flour! The recipe I give here shows you how to mimic freeze-and-bake-style cookies. Use your choice of flavored chips for desired cookie.

1 cup butter (250 grams), room temperature

½ cup (115 grams) dark or light brown sugar

½ cup (100 grams) white sugar

3 eggs

2 teaspoons Cook's powdered vanilla

3 cups (375 grams) rice flour

1 teaspoon salt

1 teaspoon baking soda

2–3 cups (350–525 grams) semisweet chocolate, milk chocolate, butterscotch (make sure they are gluten-free), or white chocolate chips

1. With a mixer, combine the butter and sugars; cream for 2 minutes. With mixer on low, add eggs one at a time and cream until smooth. Scrape down the sides of the bowl and add the vanilla. Mix again for about 10 seconds.

2. Add in flour, salt, and baking soda. Turn mixer on medium speed and blend until dough is all combined. Remove bowl from mixer and stir in desired amount of chocolate chips.

3. Firmly pack cookie dough in a 1- to 2-inch size (ice cream) scoop, and place cookies next to each other on a lined baking

SUGAR NOT ONLY adds sweetness to your baked goods, but it also adds color and tenderness, acts as a creaming agent with fats, acts as a foaming agent with eggs, and increases the keeping quality of the baked good by retaining moisture.

sheet. Depending on size of cookies, you may need two baking sheets. Place sheet in freezer and freeze for 30 minutes. Remove from baking sheet and place in a freezer bag and refreeze for up to 2 months.

4. To bake cookies, heat oven to 350°F (180°C). Take out desired amount of cookies and place on a baking sheet. Bring cookies to room temperature, about 15 minutes. You may put them in the refrigerator. Bake for 8 minutes. Leave on baking sheet until cooled completely. Remove to a cooling rack and let set for about an hour. Cookies should be able to hold their shape. Store in a covered container.

Variations: For Citrus White Chip cookies, use white chocolate chips and 2 teaspoons of lemon or orange zest.

Try replacing ½ cup (125 grams) of the butter with ½ cup (115 grams) of cream cheese. You get a zippy, fluffy, yummy cookie.

For a stuffed cookie, we like to use ½ cup (90 grams) each of semisweet chocolate, milk chocolate, white chocolate, and butterscotch chips.

Dairy-Free Variation: Use ½ cup (125 grams) shortening and ½ cup (125 grams) margarine instead of butter. Use Ener-G chocolate chips.

Egg-Free Variation: Use 3 eggs' worth of Ener-G Egg Replacer.

Low-Sugar Variation: Omit sugar and use 1 cup Whey Low. Try using unsweetened carob chips in place of chocolate.

Mini-Chip Meringues
Makes about 30

Omit the chocolate chips and try different flavored gluten-free extracts and add food coloring for fun meringues. These are more like marshmallow cookies; for crunchy meringues, turn off the oven and leave the cookies in for 4 hours.

2 large egg whites

¼ teaspoon cream of tartar

⅔ cup (140 grams) finely granulated sugar

¼ teaspoon powdered vanilla

1 cup (175 grams) mini chocolate chips

1. With a mixer on high speed, using the paddle attachment, beat egg whites and cream of tarter until thick and foamy. Gradually add the sugar and beat until mixture is stiff and has shiny peaks.

2. Remove bowl and, by hand, stir in powdered vanilla. Fold in the chocolate chips. If using a pastry bag, use the ½-inch star tube. Or, use a large zipper-lock bag and cut off a small tip on a bottom corner. Pipe out 1-inch-wide mounds about 1 inch apart on a parchment-lined baking sheet.

3. Bake in a 275°F (140°C) oven for about 30 to 35 minutes. Let cool for 5 minutes, then lift the parchment up under the cookie and pop the cookie off. Set on a cooling rack.

Variation: Use ¼ teaspoon mint, almond, or cinnamon extract. For color, add a few drops of desired food coloring when adding the sugar.

Egg-Free Variation: Try Yummy Crunchies (see facing page).

Low-Sugar Variation: Omit sugar and chocolate chips. Use ⅔ cup Whey Low.

FOR MERINGUE SHAPES, omit chocolate chips and set aside. After following recipe, put all of the meringue in a pastry bag, with optional star tip, and pipe out different shapes, letters, or critters. We like to make snakes by piping out the letter S. Do not make them bigger than 4 inches long. Bake in a 300°F (150°C) oven for about 6 minutes or until golden. Decorate with melted chocolate.

I USE HALF the amount of sugar in my recipes and still get fabulous results. You can substitute natural products for sugar like honey, fruit juice, juice concentrate, pure maple syrup, Whey Low, and rice syrup (look for one without barley). You can look for all-natural sweeteners like Sucanat, stevia, xylitol, and lohan in health food stores.

Yummy Crunchies
Makes 30

This is the perfect eggless crunch cookie—obviously named by my children! There are so many variations that you can do with these. Even if you can have eggs, this is a yummy cookie you should try.

1¼ cups butter (310 grams)

1 teaspoon dry egg replacer (optional)

2 cups (400 grams) sugar

2½ cups (310 grams) rice flour

1½ cups (185 grams) potato starch

1 teaspoon baking powder

2 teaspoons powdered vanilla

¼ teaspoon salt

2 cups (140 grams) flaked coconut

1½ cups (265 grams) chocolate pieces (optional)

½ cup (60 grams) chopped nuts (optional)

1. Cream butter, egg replacer, and sugar in a mixer. In a separate bowl, mix the flour, starch, baking powder, vanilla, and salt. Add to butter mixture and mix until you have a smooth dough. Remove from mixer and stir in by hand the remaining ingredients.

2. Drop by heaping teaspoons full of dough on a baking sheet and flatten with your hand. Bake in a 350°F (180°C) oven for 8 minutes. Cool slightly and remove to a cooling rack with a spatula.

Variation: For a holiday cookie, omit chocolate and nuts and add 1 cup (150 grams) dried cranberries and 1 teaspoon lemon zest.

Dairy-Free Variation: Replace butter with half margarine and half shortening.

Nut-Free Variation: Omit nuts.

Just Like Nilla Wafers
Makes 40

The flavor of this biscuit is scrumptious and amazingly just like Nilla Wafers! Freeze half of the baked biscuits for crumbs for your pie crusts.

1 cup (250 grams) butter, room temperature

1 cup (200 grams) sugar

1 egg

2 teaspoons powdered vanilla

1 cup (125 grams) white rice flour

1 cup (125 grams) potato starch

1. In a mixer cream together the butter and the sugar. Beat in egg and vanilla. Add the flour and starch and cream for 1 minute. Chill dough in the refrigerator.

2. Roll dough into ½-inch balls. Place on a baking sheet and flatten slightly. Bake in a 375°F (190°C) oven for about 8 minutes. Let sit on baking sheet for 5 minutes. Transfer to a cooling rack. Repeat with remaining dough. Store in a covered container.

Variation: You may use this dough in your cookie press for spritz cookies. Make sure the dough is well chilled so the cookie holds its shape.

Dairy-Free Variation: Replace butter with ½ margarine and ½ shortening.

Egg-Free Variation: Use 1 egg's worth of Ener-G Egg Replacer.

Low-Sugar Variation: Replace sugar with Whey Low.

Brown Sugar Dough
Makes about 3 cups

This dough is perfect for sweet tarts, pastries, and bar cookie bases.

¾ cup (185 grams) butter

2¼ cups (280 grams) rice flour

1¼ cups (285 grams) brown sugar, packed

½ teaspoon vanilla

¼ cup (30 grams) cornstarch

¼ teaspoon salt

8 teaspoons milk

2 egg yolks

1. In a food processor, combine butter, half of the flour, and the sugar. Pulse until the mixture resembles cornmeal.

2. Add all remaining ingredients and process until dough forms a ball and comes together. If needed, carefully pull dough apart and place in processor to blend again until you get smooth dough.

3. Remove dough from processor and divide in half. Wrap in wax paper and chill until ready to use.

Dairy-Free Variation: Replace milk with soy or rice milk. Replace butter with equal amounts of margarine or shortening.

Egg-Free Variation: Substitute eggs with 2 teaspoons Ener-G Egg Replacer.

Low-Sugar Variation: Omit brown sugar and replace with 1 cup Whey Low.

Fruit Bars
Makes 20 bars

This is the perfect sweet for those who do not want chocolate. They freeze well. My baby likes to eat them frozen! Sometimes we eat them in the morning while other kids are eating Pop-Tarts.

1 cup Brown Sugar Dough

½ cup (60 grams) rice flour

1 cup (100 grams) oats or buckwheat flakes, divided

¼ cup (30 grams) cornstarch

¼ teaspoon cinnamon

½ cup (125 grams) butter, cut into pieces

¼ teaspoon baking soda

1 10.25-ounce (290-gram) jar low-sugar jam, such as apricot, strawberry, or blackberry

1. Press chilled dough into a 9-inch × 9-inch × 2-inch jam sponge roll tin. Wet your hands if dough is too sticky. Bake in a 350°F (180°C) oven for 10 minutes. Remove and set aside to cool.

2. In a food processor, add flour, ½ cup (50 grams) oats, cornstarch, cinnamon, and butter.

3. Pulse mixture until it resembles pieces the size of peas.

4. Add baking soda and ½ cup (50 grams) oats and pulse mixture quickly 3 or 4 times.

5. Spread preserves onto cooled crust.

6. Sprinkle strudel topping all over the preserves. Bake for 30 to 35 minutes or until golden on top. Cool one hour or until room temperature. Cover and place in the refrigerator. When chilled, cut into bars and serve, or wrap and freeze.

Dairy-Free Variation: *Use margarine in place of butter.*

GLUTEN IS OFTEN found in caramel-flavored syrups. Make this caramel recipe and store it in a plastic container for up to 2 weeks, and use it to create homemade ice-cream sundaes!

Who Wants a Twix-y Bar?
Makes 16 bars

This is a treat that I missed out on as a kid, but you do not have to!

1½ cups Brown Sugar Dough (page 159)

10 teaspoons butter

3 tablespoons brown sugar

1 14-ounce (400-gram) can condensed milk

1 cup (175 grams) semisweet or milk chocolate chips

1. In a 9-inch square cake pan, press dough in evenly and prick with a fork.

2. Bake in a 375°F (190°C) oven for 20 minutes, or until lightly golden. Remove and let cool in the pan.

3. To make the caramel, place the butter, sugar, and condensed milk in a nonstick saucepan and cook over medium-low heat until the mixture comes to a boil. Reduce the heat and cook for 4-5 minutes until the caramel is pale golden and thick and is coming away from the sides of the pan. Pour the topping over the shortbread base and let cool.

4. In a microwave-safe bowl, melt the chocolate according to the package directions. When the caramel topping is firm, place it into the refrigerator to cool completely. Remove and cut the cookies into long rectangles, or finger-size shapes. Place cookies on a parchment-lined baking sheet and pour chocolate over each cookie until all are completely covered with chocolate. Put back into refrigerator to cool. Serve, or wrap in parchment and freeze in a zipper-lock bag. They taste great frozen, too!

Coconut Wheels
Makes about 20 sandwiches

My girls like to roll the wheels in the coconut for me. If your kids do not like coconut, you can omit it and have yummy caramel cookies. Or have your child roll cookie wheels in colored sugar—sweet but fun!

2 cups Brown Sugar Dough (page 159)

Caramel recipe from Who Wants a Twix-y Bar? (see page 161), cooled

1 cup (70 grams) flaked coconut

1. Divide dough into two discs and put between two oil-sprayed pieces of wax paper. Roll out to ⅛ of an inch thick. With a 2- or 3-inch round biscuit cutter, cut out cookies. Gather scraps of dough and repeat process until all dough has been used. If cookies start sticking, spray with cooking oil. Place 1 inch apart on a greased baking tray. Bake in a 350°F (180°C) oven for about 10 minutes. Remove cookies to rack to cool.

2. Turn cookies bottom-side up and spread 1 tablespoon caramel on half of the cookies. Sandwich together with remaining cookies.

3. Fill a small bowl with coconut. Squeeze the cookie slightly so it oozes out a little caramel and roll in the coconut. Repeat with all cookies.

Variation: Decorate with melted chocolate designs for a gourmet holiday cookie.

Dairy-Free Variation: Fill with dairy-free icing.

VANILLA IS ONE of the most popular flavorings in dessert making. It is derived from aromatic pods of a variety of orchid. The extract, or essence, is made by dissolving the essential oil of the vanilla bean in an alcohol base. Use products labeled "pure" or "natural" powdered vanilla. Extract from Madagascar has the best quality. "Essence" is not the same thing. Powdered vanilla is very useful for sauces, custards, and a million-and-one sweet dishes or wherever a touch of vanilla flavor is required. I always double the vanilla in all my recipes for added flavor.

Easy Multipurpose Sugar Cookie Dough
Makes about 3 cups

Take your pick of which yummy treat to create.

½ cup (60 grams) powdered sugar

½ cup (100 grams) granulated sugar

1 cup butter (250 grams), cut into small pieces

1 3-ounce (85-gram) package cream cheese, cut in thirds

2¾ cups (340 grams) white rice flour, divided

2 eggs

2 teaspoons powdered vanilla

¼ cup (30 grams) cornstarch

¼ teaspoon salt

1. In a food processor, add sugars, butter, cream cheese, and 1 cup (125 grams) flour. Process until mixture resembles pea-size crumbs.

2. Add remaining ingredients and process until well combined.

3. Remove to wax paper, wrap, and chill for an hour or so.

Dairy-Free Variation: *Replace butter with 1 cup shortening and cream cheese with 3 ounces soy cream cheese.*

Egg-Free Variation: *Cream together dry Ener-G Egg Replacer and water to equal two eggs.*

Low-Sugar Variation: *Replace sugars with 1 cup Whey Low.*

Chocolate Kiss Cookies
Makes about 24

> 2 cups Sugar Cookie Dough (page 169) or
>   Fun Cut-Outs dough (page 166)
> 1 bag Hershey's Chocolate Kisses, unwrapped

1. Using chilled dough, make about eight 2-tablespoon-size balls. Spread out on a baking tray.

2. Push a chocolate kiss into each dough ball.

3. Bake at 350°F (180°C) for 6–8 minutes until barely golden around the base of the cookie. Let cool on the baking tray before removing. Repeat with remaining dough until all Hershey's Kisses are gone.

Variation: Melt white chocolate, butterscotch, mint, or peanut butter-flavored chips in the microwave according to package directions. With each cookie ball, push an indentation in and fill with melted chocolate. To make Thumbprints, fill each indentation with jam. Bake accordingly. If allowed to have nuts, roll each cookie in finely chopped almonds or peanuts before baking.

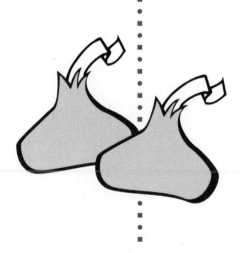

HERE'S A FUN IDEA. Make your shortbread flavor of choice in the springform pan. When completely cooled, frost with frosting or instant pudding and top with fruits, candies, and fun sprinkles to make a yummy Cookie Pizza.

Shortbread
Serves 6

1½ cups Sugar Cookie Dough (page 169) or
Tea Cake dough (page 167) (omit nuts if desired)

1. For triangle wedges, push dough into a springform pan. Pierce with a fork and sprinkle with a little sugar. Bake in a preheated 325°F (170°C) oven for 30 minutes, or until firm. Let cool for 10 minutes. Run a knife along the edge of the biscuit and remove rim of the springform pan. Carefully cut into wedges like a pizza. Place biscuit circle in the refrigerator to chill.

2. For biscuits, roll a small handful of dough into balls or "fat snakes." Gently flatten slightly. Sprinkle with your choice of granulated sugar, or leave plain. Bake on a baking tray at 350°F (180°C) for about 8 minutes.

Variation: For chocolate shortbread, let the dough come to room temperature and place into food processor. Melt 2 ounces (55 grams) of semisweet chocolate according to package directions. Pour onto dough and process until even in color. Bake accordingly.

Fun Cut-Outs
Makes about 24

These taste great and are perfect for school parties and special occasions like Halloween, Valentine's Day, and Easter.

1 5-ounce (140-gram) box instant vanilla pudding (optional flavor, see sidebar*)

½ cup milk or water

½ cup (125 grams) butter or shortening

½ cup (100 grams) sugar

3 eggs

3½ cups (430 grams) rice flour

½ teaspoon baking soda

½ teaspoon baking powder

½ teaspoon salt

Royal Icing (page 207)

Sprinkles, candies, or colored sugars

1. In a mixer, cream together the box of pudding and milk. Let sit for 5 minutes. Add butter and the sugar; blend until smooth. Add eggs and mix, scraping down the sides.

2. Add the flour, baking soda, baking powder, and salt. Blend on medium speed until well incorporated.

3. Divide dough in thirds. Chill in the freezer or refrigerator. Take one disk of dough and place on a large piece of wax paper sprayed with oil. Spray dough and cover with wax paper. Roll out to desired biscuit-cutter thickness. Use biscuit cutters, working one section at a time. If dough gets too sticky, re-chill and spray dough and biscuit cutter with cooking oil.

4. Bake at 350°F (180°C) for 6–8 minutes depending on the size of the cookie. Remove from oven and let cookies cool on baking tray before removing to cooling rack. You may freeze dough for up to one month.

5. Once cookies are cool, you may decorate them with frosting and sprinkles. Store in a covered container in the refrigerator.

FOR GINGERBREAD cookies, omit sugar and use ½ cup (110 grams) dark brown sugar. Add 1½ teaspoons ginger and 1 teaspoon cinnamon with the flour.

YOU CAN ALSO make an interesting cookie by using any instant pudding flavor you desire. Make sure to read the ingredients for hidden allergens. Pistachio-flavored pudding plus a few drops of green dye make a fun St. Patrick's Day cookie! Chocolate-flavored pudding cookies are great for Halloween and parties. Be creative!

Dairy-Free Variation: *Use Easy Multipurpose Sugar Cookie Dough (see page 163).*

Egg-Free Variation: *Use 3 eggs' worth of Ener-G Egg Replacer.*

VIRTUALLY EVERY culture has its version of sugar cookies. Arab countries decorate the cookies with a pistachio or almond in the center of each, Greeks put a clove as a decoration, and many cultures heavily dust the top with powdered sugar. No matter where you're from or how you decorate them, sugar cookies are a favorite.

Tea Cakes
Makes 40

This is my favorite biscuit. I think this is better than the wheat version.

1 cup (150 grams) pecans
½ cup (125 grams) butter
½ cup (125 grams) shortening
2 teaspoons Ener-G Egg Replacer plus 1 tablespoon water
1 cup (120 grams) powdered sugar, divided
2 teaspoons powdered vanilla
¼ teaspoon salt
2 cups (250 grams) rice flour

1. In a food processor add pecans and pulse until finely chopped.

2. In a mixer cream together the butter, shortening, egg replacer, and water. Add ½ cup (60 grams) powdered sugar, vanilla, and salt. Cream together until smooth. Mix in the rice flour and the pecans. Chill dough until firm.

3. With the cold, firm dough make 1- to 3-inch balls. Place them 2 inches apart on a baking sheet lined with parchment or tinfoil. Bake in a 350°F (180°C) oven until lightly browned on the sides. Remove the parchment with biscuits on it to a flat surface. Let biscuits cool completely.

4. Place remaining powdered sugar in a large, deep bowl. Roll each biscuit in the sugar. Store, covered, up to 1 week.

Dairy-Free Variation: Omit butter; replace with margarine.

Low-Sugar Variation: Replace sugar with 1 cup Whey Low.

Nut-Free Variation: Omit pecans and replace with 1 cup (130 grams) grated chocolate or 2 tablespoons lemon zest.

Crinkle Crunchies
Makes 16

These flourless cookies are very simple to make and they travel well.

1 cup (175 grams) semisweet chocolate chips
1¾ cups (250 grams) almonds
⅓ cup (70 grams) sugar
1 teaspoon powdered vanilla
2 egg whites

1. Place the chocolate in a food processor and process until coarsely chopped. Add the almonds and the sugar; process until mixture is finely ground. Add vanilla and egg whites; process just until mixture forms moist dough.

2. Form 1-inch balls and place 2 inches apart on a parchment- or tinfoil-lined baking tray. Bake in a 350°F (180°C) oven for 8 minutes. Remove from oven and let rest 5 minutes on baking tray. Remove cookie to cooling rack and cool completely. Store in an airtight container for up to 2 weeks.

Variation: Replace the dark chocolate with equal amounts of white chocolate.

Egg-Free Variation: Use 2 eggs' worth of Ener-G Egg Replacer.

Nut-Free Variation: Omit almonds and add 1¾ (125 grams) cups shredded coconut.

LOOKING FOR non-hydrogenated products? Spectrum makes a great line of baking goods like margarine, shortening, and oils. Have your store order some today!

CREAM OF TARTAR is a natural, pure ingredient left behind after grape juice has fermented to wine. It is obtained from wine-producing regions. Cream of tartar is used to stabilize egg white foam. It is also a major ingredient in baking powder. Cream of tartar has no aroma and has an acidic flavor.

Sugar Cookie Dough
Makes 24

This is an old-fashioned favorite that my family loves. If you keep the dough well chilled and really work with it, these rolled-out cookies are delicate and delicious. I prefer this dough made dairy-free and egg-free.

½ cup (125 grams) butter

1 cup (200 grams) sugar

1 egg

1 teaspoon powdered vanilla

1½ cups (185 grams) white rice flour

¼ teaspoon baking soda

¼ teaspoon cream of tartar

Colored sugar for sprinkling or cookie sprinkles

1. In a mixer with the paddle attachment, cream together the butter and sugar. Add the egg and vanilla; blend, scraping down sides. Add the flour, baking soda, and cream of tartar. Blend until combined. Chill dough.

2. Place the colored sugar in a bowl. Roll out 1- to 2-inch balls with chilled dough. Dip each ball in the colored sugar. Place balls 4 inches apart from each other on a baking tray lined with parchment or tinfoil; flatten cookies slightly. Bake in a 375°F (190°C) oven for 10 minutes. Cool slightly on baking tray and lift off parchment and place on a flat surface to cool completely. Store in an airtight container for 1 week.

Variation: For Snicker Doodles, roll cookie in a mixture of ¼ cup (50 grams) coarse sugar and 1 teaspoon cinnamon. Or, try pushing 3 or 4 M&M's into each cookie.

Dairy-Free Variation: Use ¼ cup (60 grams) margarine and ¼ cup (60 grams) shortening.

Egg-Free Variation: Omit eggs and cream together 1 teaspoon Ener-G Egg Replacer and 1 tablespoon water with the butter.

Low-Sugar Variation: Use Whey Low.

Lemon Berry Bars
Makes 16 bars

My aunt loves lemon bars, and she totally approves of these!

2 sticks butter

½ cup (60 grams) powdered sugar

1 teaspoon powdered vanilla

1¾ cups (215 grams) rice flour

⅓ cup (40 grams) cornstarch

2 tablespoons lemon juice

4 eggs

1 cup (200 grams) sugar

2 teaspoons grated lemon peel

⅓ cup lemon juice

½ teaspoon baking powder

⅛ teaspoon salt

1½ cups (220 grams) fresh blueberries or raspberries

1. In a food processor add the butter, flour, and the sugar; whirl together. Add the cornstarch, vanilla, and lemon juice. Process until the dough comes together in a ball. Press into a 9-inch × 13-inch pan. Bake in a 350°F (180°C) oven for 15 minutes.

2. In a large bowl mix together the eggs, sugar, lemon juice and peel, salt, and baking powder. Pour into the crust and sprinkle the berries evenly over it. Return back to the oven and bake for 25 minutes more. Remove and let cool for 30 minutes. Sift additional powdered sugar over the top. Cut into bars. Serve warm or cold. Store covered in the refrigerator.

Dairy-Free Variation: Use margarine.

Egg-Free Variation: Replace with 4 eggs' worth of Ener-G Egg Replacer and water.

Low-Sugar Variation: Omit sugars. Use 1½ cups of Whey Low.

THE CLEAN, refreshing taste of lemon bars makes them a perfect treat during summer. They also make great gifts for aunties and grandmas when wrapped in cellophane on a pretty dish.

FOR THOSE SUFFERING with nut allergies, try this without nuts. But for those without nut allergies, it's like bites of pecan pie. Nutritionally, ¼ cup (40 grams) of pecans actually provides 4 percent of one's daily requirement of iron. If you or your children need to eat more iron-rich foods, you might try offering a few pecans!

Pecan Sweets
Makes 36 bars

These delicious cookie bars taste just like sweets. Kids of all ages love these!

2 cups Brown Sugar Dough (page 159)

3 eggs

½ cup (100 grams) sugar

1⅓ cups (455 grams) light corn syrup

2 tablespoons (30 grams) butter, melted

4 ounces (115 grams) semisweet chocolate, melted

1 teaspoon powdered vanilla

1½ cups (185 grams) chopped pecans

1. Press the dough into a greased 13-inch × 9-inch baking pan and bake in a 350°F (180°C) oven for 12 minutes.

2. Meanwhile, beat together the eggs, sugar, corn syrup, butter, chocolate, and vanilla. Stir in the pecans. Pour over baked crust.

3. Bake in a 350°F (180°C) oven for about 30 minutes. Remove and let cool completely before cutting into bars. You may dust with powdered sugar if desired. These taste delicious cold. Keep covered in the refrigerator.

Dairy-Free Variation: Use margarine, and Ener-G semisweet chocolate.

Egg-Free Variation: Replace with 3 eggs' worth of Ener-G Egg Replacer and water.

Nut-Free Variation: Omit nuts.

Apple Rice Pudding
Serves 6

This is very rich, creamy, and delicious. Best of all, this is great whether served warm or cold.

2 12-ounce (340-gram) cans evaporated milk, divided

2 cups water

1 cup (200 grams) small-grain white rice

1 teaspoon vanilla

1 teaspoon cinnamon

Pinch of salt

A little less than ½ cup (100 grams) sugar

1 tablespoon brown sugar

1½ cups (225 grams) finely chopped apples
   (about 2 apples)

2 egg yolks

Caramel recipe (optional) (page 188)

1. In a medium saucepan combine 2 cups (1½ cans) of evaporated milk, 2 cups water, rice, vanilla, cinnamon, salt, and sugars. Cook at a gentle simmer over medium heat, stirring occasionally. Cook for about 20 minutes. When most of the liquid has been absorbed, add in the apples. Cook about 10 more minutes. In a large bowl, whisk together the remaining evaporated milk with the egg yolks. Gradually stir into the rice mixture. Cook over medium heat, stirring constantly, until mixture boils and thickens, about 10 minutes.

2. Spoon into individual bowls and drizzle caramel sauce over.

Dairy-Free Variation: Replace milk with 3 cups soy or rice milk.

Egg-Free Variation: Omit eggs.

Low-Sugar Variation: Omit sugar.

SO MANY TIMES, we think of wheat as the "staff of life," but did you know that most of the world's population sits down to a rice meal during the day?

RICE PUDDING VARIATIONS:

For raisin pudding, omit apples and add 1 cup (150 grams) raisins.

For chocolate rice pudding, add in ⅔ cup (120 grams) chocolate chips in place of the apples. Omit the cinnamon and brown sugar. Stir until the chocolate chips are melted.

For plain pudding, omit apples, brown sugar, and cinnamon. Increase the vanilla by 2 teaspoons and add ¼ cup (50 grams) sugar.

DID YOU KNOW that raisins, sultanas, and currants are all dried grapes. Raisins come in many different shapes and sizes depending upon the grape the dried bit started out as. Originally, most raisins hailed from Turkey and the Mediterranean, but today most raisins come from California.

Low/No Sugar Baked Rice Pudding
Serves 5

The key to the sweetness here is to add nutmeg. This treat also makes an excellent breakfast.

4 eggs
2 cups milk
2 cups (330 grams) rice, cooked
¼ cup (50 grams) sugar (optional)
2 tablespoons (30 grams) butter, melted
2 teaspoons lemon zest
¼ teaspoon nutmeg
1 tablespoon lemon juice
½ cup (75 grams) golden raisins

1. In a large bowl, whisk together eggs and milk. Add the remaining ingredients. Pour into a buttered glass pie dish.
2. Bake in a 350°F (180°C) oven for 45 minutes. Cool and serve warm or chill and serve cold.

Dairy-Free Variation: Replace milk with equal amount of rice or soy milk, and butter with margarine.

Egg-Free Variation: Omit eggs and mix ⅓ cup (40 grams) Ener-G Egg Replacer with ⅓ cup water; add to the milk.

Oatmeal Raisin
Makes 16

⅓ cup (85 grams) shortening

1 stick butter

1½ cups (330 grams) brown sugar

2 eggs

1½ cups (185 grams) rice flour

1 teaspoon cinnamon

1 teaspoon baking soda

2 teaspoons vanilla

1¾ cups (175 grams) rolled oats or buckwheat flakes

2 cups (300 grams) raisins

1. In a mixer cream together the shortening, butter, sugar, and the eggs. Add the flour, cinnamon, baking soda, and vanilla. Blend until combined. Stir in the oats and raisins. Drop onto a tinfoil-lined baking tray. Bake in a 350°F (180°C) oven for 10 minutes. Let cool slightly, lift up foil and place on a flat surface to cool completely. When completely cooled, peel off foil and place in an airtight container for up to 2 weeks.

Dairy-Free Variation: Use shortening, oil, or margarine instead of butter.

Egg-Free Variation: Omit egg and add 1 tablespoon Ener-G Egg Replacer.

Low-Sugar Variation: Replace brown sugar with Whey Low.

ONE DRIED FRUIT often neglected is the date. Dates are a popular snack and cake addition in Europe and have been an important part of the diet of people in Northern Africa and the Middle East for centuries. When shopping for dates, look for moist, plump fruits. Try using dates in this recipe for a new flavor.

Vegan Chip Cookies
Makes 30

These are surprisingly good little biscuit cookies. You may add a teaspoon of cinnamon or orange zest if desired.

1 cup (250 grams) applesauce

¼ cup (55 grams) brown sugar (optional)

¼ cup (50 grams) white sugar (optional)

2½ cups (310 grams) rice flour

1 teaspoon salt

1 teaspoon baking soda

1 teaspoon baking powder

2 cups (350 grams) chocolate chips, carob chips, raisins, dates, or other dried fruit

1. In a mixer, cream together the applesauce and the sugars. Add the dry ingredients and blend well. Stir in the chocolate chips or dried fruit.

2. Drop 2-inch mounds onto a greased baking tray. Bake in a 350°F (180°C) oven for about 8 minutes or until firm. Cool completely on the baking tray. Store in a covered container.

Low-Sugar Variation: Omit sugar.

Mini Zebra Bites
Makes about 50

This is a mini-cookie with giant chocolate and white chocolate flavors.

1¼ cups (310 grams) butter, room temperature

2 cups (400 grams) white sugar

2 eggs

2 teaspoons powdered vanilla

2 cups (250 grams) rice flour

¾ cup (90 grams) Nestlé cocoa powder, unsweetened

1 teaspoon baking soda

½ teaspoon salt

2 cups (350 grams) white chocolate chips

1. In a mixer with the paddle attachment, cream the butter until fluffy. Add the sugar, eggs, and the vanilla; beat 1 minute. Beat on low until combined the flour, cocoa, baking soda, and salt. Stir in the white chocolate chips.

2. Form 1-inch balls and place on a baking tray. Flatten slightly. Bake in a 350°F (180°C) oven for 5 to 6 minutes. They will puff slightly while baking and flatten when cooled. Cool slightly and remove to a cooling rack to cool completely.

Dairy-Free Variation: Use margarine instead of butter.

Egg-Free Variation: Omit eggs; replace with 2 eggs' worth of Ener-G Egg Replacer.

Low-Sugar Variation: Omit white chips. Use 2 cups Whey Low in place of sugar.

LINE A SPRINGFORM pan with Little Fingers; layer with pudding, fresh fruit, grated chocolate, and whipped cream. Repeat layers three times. Chill for 4 hours, remove rim, and serve a delicious Berrimisu!

Little Fingers
Makes 20

Your basic "Ladyfingers" cookie but made for little fingers.

6 eggs, separated
¾ cup (150 grams) sugar, divided
1 teaspoon powdered vanilla
¼ teaspoon cream of tartar
¾ cup (90 grams) white rice flour
½ cup (60 grams) cornstarch
½ teaspoon salt
Powdered sugar for sprinkling

1. In a mixer blend together the egg yolks, ¼ cup sugar, and vanilla for 4 minutes. Pour into a bowl and set aside.

2. In a clean bowl with the paddle attachment, whip the egg whites, ¼ cup sugar, and cream of tartar until soft peaks form. Gradually add remaining sugar in while machine is still running. Fold in the egg yolk mixture and the flour, cornstarch, and salt. Do not overmix.

3. Place mixture in a pastry bag with a ½-inch round tip, or in a sturdy zipper-lock bag with one corner cut off to make a ½-inch opening.

4. Pipe out 2- to 4-inch-long "fingers" onto a tinfoil-lined baking tray, 1 inch apart. Bake in a 425°F (220°C) oven for 4 to 8 minutes, depending on the size of the cookie. Remove and let cool on the baking tray. Lift up the tinfoil and remove to counter. Gently peel off cookie and place on a cooling rack. Sprinkle with powdered sugar. Return to a warm oven and toast for an additional 10 minutes. Cool. Store in an airtight container.

Low-Sugar Variation: Replace with ¾ cup Whey Low.

My Madelines
Makes about 12

Madeleines are little shell-shaped cookies that are dainty and buttery. My little Madeline likes to eat our version while we go shopping! You may add 2 teaspoons of lemon zest to mixture if desired. If you do not have a madeleine pan, use mixture for bar cookies.

4 eggs, room temperature

¼ teaspoon salt

⅔ cup (80 grams) powdered sugar

1 cup (125 grams) rice flour

1 teaspoon powdered vanilla

½ cup (125 grams) butter, very soft

1. In a mixer with the paddle attachment, beat the eggs, salt, and the sugar until very fluffy, almost 8 minutes. Fold in the flour, vanilla, and the butter.

2. Grease well your shell or madeleine mold. Spoon mixture into each shell, filling to the top. Bake in a 375°F (190°C) oven for 8 minutes or until golden. Quickly remove from mold; you can use a butter knife to gently lift out. Let cool on a rack. Sprinkle with powdered sugar, or dip half in melted chocolate.

Dairy-Free Variation: *Use margarine.*

Low-Sugar Variation: *Replace powdered sugar with Whey Low.*

SPECIALTY COOKIES are cookies that get their distinct, well-defined shapes from special tools. French madeleines are baked in madeleine plaques; spicy Dutch speculaas are pressed into carved wooden molds; Swedish spritz cookies are formed into wreaths, ribbons, rosettes, and other shapes using a cookie press fitted with a decorative template; German springerle are formed using a special carved rolling pin. The dough is stamped with the design, cut out, and then allowed to dry overnight to set the design before the cookies are baked.

THE WORD COOKIE comes from the Dutch *koekje,* meaning "little cake." Most cookies, however, are much more like sweetened pastry than like cake. Unlike both cake and pastry, they are very easy to make in the food processor, electric mixer, or by hand the way our grandmothers used to do. The earliest cookie-style cakes are thought to date back to seventh-century Persia, one of the first countries to cultivate sugar. Each country has its own word for cookie. What we know as cookies are called biscuits in England; in Spain they're *galletas,* Germans call them *keks,* Italians have their biscotti, and so on. The very first cookie was the drop cookie—a small spoonful of cake batter, baked before the cake so that the cook could judge the oven temperature and the flavor and texture of the batter.

(Source: wwwiz.com)

Frosted Brownies
Makes 10 bars

⅓ cup water

1 tablespoon corn syrup

1 cup (200 grams) sugar

½ cup (125 grams) butter

2 cups (350 grams) semisweet chocolate chips, divided

3 eggs

1 cup (125 grams) rice flour

½ teaspoon baking powder

¼ teaspoon salt

½ cup cream

½ cup (60 grams) powdered sugar

1. In a saucepan combine the water, corn syrup, sugar, and butter. Cook over medium heat, stirring constantly, until mixture comes to a boil. Remove from heat and stir in 1 cup chocolate chips. Stir until smooth and cool, about 4 minutes. Add the eggs one at a time, stirring well after each. Stir in the flour, baking powder, and salt. Pour into a greased 9-inch square baking pan. Bake in a 350°F (180°C) oven for 30 minutes. Set aside to cool.

2. For frosting, in a small saucepan add 1 cup chocolate chips and cream and stir continually over low heat. Remove from heat and stir in the powdered sugar. Cover and place into the refrigerator until thickened. Stir again and pour over brownies. Cover brownies and return to refrigerator until set, about 1 hour. Cut into squares.

Variation: For cream-filled brownies, add 7 ounces (200 grams) cream cheese or soy cream cheese, ¼ cup (50 grams) sugar, and 1 teaspoon vanilla blended together. Pour 1/2 of the brownie mixture into pan, spread cheese mixture over, and pour remaining brownie mixture on top. Bake as usual.

Dairy-Free Variation: Use margarine, coconut milk in place of cream, and Ener-G chocolate chips.

Egg-Free Variation: Omit eggs and stir in ⅓ cup (80 grams) applesauce.

Oh Whee Ohs
Makes about 25 sandwich cookies

This is what my two-year-old calls the famous chocolate cream-filled cookies!

COOKIE:

¾ cup (180 grams) butter

1¼ cups (250 grams) sugar

⅔ cup (120 grams) semisweet chocolate, melted

2 eggs

¾ cup (90 grams) cocoa

1¼ cups (155 grams) rice flour

½ teaspoon salt

¼ teaspoon baking powder

1 teaspoon baking soda

FILLING:

¼ cup (60 grams) butter

¼ cup (60 grams) shortening

1⅔ cups (200 grams) powdered sugar

2 teaspoons powdered vanilla

1. In a mixer cream together ¾ cup butter with 1¼ cups sugar. With mixer on low slowly add the melted chocolate. Add the eggs, scraping down sides if needed. Pour in the cocoa, flour, salt, baking powder, and baking soda. Mix on low speed until combined.

FOR EASIEST and inexpensive baking, line your baking trays with tinfoil! After removing cookies from the oven, let sit for 5 minutes. When cool to the touch, lift the corners of the tinfoil up and gently lay on a flat surface to continue cooling. Simply re-line baking tray and repeat. The secret to perfect gluten-free cookies is to let them sit and cool as long as possible to prevent crumbling. This also works well for brownies and cake.

2. Using a ¼-ounce ice-cream scoop, drop dough onto a tinfoil-lined baking tray. Allow 1 inch between each cookie. Flatten slightly. Bake in a 350°F (180°C) oven for 8 minutes. Cool slightly; lift foil carefully and place on a flat surface to cool completely.

3. To make filling, in a clean mixer with a paddle attachment, cream butter and shortening until well combined. Add the powdered sugar and vanilla. Beat until fluffy, about 2 minutes.

4. To assemble, take 1 cookie and spread 1 teaspoon of filling on bottom; place one more cookie onto frosted side, bottom down. Repeat with remaining cookies.

Dairy-Free Variation: *Use margarine or shortening, and Ener-G semisweet chocolate.*

Egg-Free Variation: *Omit eggs and add 2 eggs' worth of Ener-G Egg Replacer with water.*

Low-Sugar Variation: *Replace all sugar with Whey Low.*

Marshmallow Crunchy Bar Cut-Outs
Makes 30

Take your average marshmallow/crisp rice cereal treat and jazz it up for fun!

7 cups (350 grams) mini marshmallows

⅔ cup (170 grams) butter

½ teaspoon salt

5 cups (150 grams) gluten-free rice or corn cereal
  (rice, puffed cocoa crisps, or fruit crisps)

2 teaspoons powdered vanilla

1 cup (200 grams) sweets, your choice

1. In a large pot over low heat, melt the butter, marshmallows, and salt. Stir in the cereal and the vanilla, making sure to coat each piece of cereal. Stir in candy pieces.

2. Line a baking tray with wax paper. Spread rice mixture onto wax paper; try to spread out like a rectangle. Coat your hands with cooking spray and push down the mixture into an even, flat rectangle.

3. Cool to room temperature. Spray selected biscuit cutters (like stars or teddy bears) with cooking oil and firmly cut out shapes. Remove with a spatula and place on a wax paper-lined baking tray. Decorate with frosting, melted chocolate, additional sweets, or cookie sprinkles. Royal Icing (page 207) makes beautiful cookies. You can even stick a cookie stick in the side, wrap in plastic wrap, and give as a gift or a special treat.

***Dairy-Free Variation:** Use margarine in place of butter.*

DID YOU KNOW that M&M's and Reese's Peanut Butter Cups are gluten-free? Call the company's customer service number for a list of allergen-free sweets.

Double Chocolate Pound Cake
Serves 8

This works best as a pound cake or in a Bundt pan.

1 cup (250 grams) butter

1½ (300 grams) cups sugar

4 eggs

2 teaspoons vanilla

1 cup (230 grams) sour cream

1½ cups (185 grams) rice flour

1 teaspoon baking powder

½ teaspoon salt

½ cup (60 grams) cocoa powder

1½ cups (260 grams) mini chocolate chips

1. In a mixer cream together butter and sugar until fluffy. Add eggs, vanilla, and sour cream; cream until well blended. Add the flour, baking powder, salt, and cocoa. Fold in the chocolate chips.

2. Pour batter into a greased 9-inch × 5-inch × 3-inch loaf pan. Bake in a 325°F (170°C) oven for 1 hour and 35 minutes. Cool for 15 minutes. Run knife around edges and invert onto a cooling rack. Flip over and let cool to room temperature. Serve with fresh fruit and cream.

Variation: Try using different-flavored chips like white chocolate or mint.

Dairy-Free Variation: Substitute 1 cup (250 grams) pureed silken tofu for the sour cream. Use margarine in place of butter; use Nestlé cocoa powder and Ener-G chocolate chips.

Egg-Free Variation: Omit eggs and add 1 cup (250 grams) applesauce.

Chocolate Cake
Serves 12

This cake is moist and chocolaty. This is one of my personal favorites. I've never met anyone who could tell that it is wheat-free.

½ cup water

1 cup (175 grams) semisweet chocolate chips

1 cup (250 grams) butter

1½ cups (300 grams) sugar

5 eggs, separated

1 teaspoon powdered vanilla

⅓ cup (40 grams) cocoa powder

2 cups (250 grams) rice flour

1 teaspoon baking soda

1 teaspoon baking powder

1 cup buttermilk (or milk)

1. In a small saucepan, bring the water and the chocolate chips to a boil. Remove from heat and continue stirring until you have a smooth syrup.

2. In a mixer cream the butter and the sugar. Add the egg yolks and blend. Pour in the chocolate syrup and the vanilla; mix until smooth.

3. Add the cocoa, rice flour, baking soda, and baking powder. Blend on low speed. Slowly pour in the buttermilk, while mixer is mixing. Blend until smooth, scraping down the sides.

4. In a clean mixing bowl add the egg whites and whip until you have firm peaks. By hand, slowly incorporate the chocolate mixture into the egg whites.

5. Pour batter into 2 greased cake pans lined with parchment. Bake in a 350°F (180°C) oven for 30 minutes, or until firm in the middle. Remove and let cool for 30 minutes before inverting onto a cooling rack and removing the parchment paper. Cool again until cake is at room temperature. Frost with desired frosting.

Dairy-Free Variation: *Use canola oil or margarine in place of butter. Use buttermilk substitute or water in place of buttermilk. Use Nestlé cocoa powder and Ener-G chocolate chips.*

Egg-Free Variation: *Omit eggs. Simply cream together 1 cup (250 grams) applesauce or ½ cup oil with sugar/butter mixture. Omit step 4.*

Low-Sugar Variation: *Replace sugar with Whey Low.*

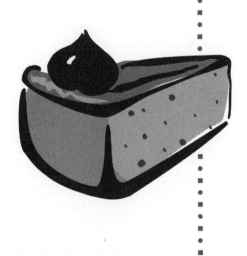

 ## Carrot Cake
Serves 10

These also make perfect cupcakes.

½ cup (100 grams) sugar

¾ cup oil

4 eggs

1 teaspoon powdered vanilla

2 cups (250 grams) rice flour

2 teaspoons baking powder

1 teaspoon baking soda

1 teaspoon cinnamon

1 teaspoon ginger

2 cups (220 grams) shredded carrots

½ cup (60 grams) chopped pecans (optional)

1 8-ounce (225-gram) can crushed pineapple, drained

1. In a mixer, blend together the sugar, oil, eggs, and vanilla. Add the flour, baking powder, baking soda, cinnamon, and ginger. Blend in the shredded carrots, nuts, and the crushed pineapple.
2. Pour batter into two cake pans lined with parchment paper, and bake in a 350°F (180°C) oven for 40 minutes or until firm in the center. Let cool for 25 minutes and then invert onto a cooling rack. Peel off the parchment paper. Cool for an additional 20 minutes or until cake is room temperature. Frost as desired.

For cupcakes, fill 24 paper-lined muffin tins. Bake for 15 minutes.

Egg-Free Variation: *Use ½ cup (125 grams) applesauce when creaming the oil.*

Low-Sugar Variation: *Use ½ cup of the pineapple juice and omit sugar.*

Nut-Free Variation: *Omit nuts.*

BAKING SODA is the chemical sodium bicarbonate. If moisture and something acidic like honey, molasses, buttermilk, brown sugar, fruit juice, or chocolate is mixed with the baking soda, carbon dioxide gas is released, which leavens the baked good. Use mixture at once or the gases will escape and your baked good won't rise!

EGGS ARE HIGH in fat and protein. They contain several vitamins and iron. If not allergic to eggs, they can be the gluten-free baker's best friend! Like gluten, egg protein coagulates to give structure to baked products. Beaten eggs make tiny bubbles in a batter and help leaven your product. They also contribute to flavor, color, and moisture. If allergic to eggs, I have found Ener-G Egg Replacer does an excellent job replacing the eggs' function!

Creamsicle Cake
Serves 12

This fun cake was featured in the Sacramento Bee *newspaper. Everyone who tried it said it was fabulous. I make this on the 4th of July and decorate it with blueberries in the shape of a star. It also makes a wonderful birthday cake.*

6 eggs, room temperature
½ cup orange juice
2 teaspoons powdered vanilla
1 cup (120 grams) powdered sugar
1¼ cups (155 grams) white rice flour
½ teaspoon cream of tartar
3 tablespoons sugar

1. In a mixer beat egg yolks until lemon colored, about 4 minutes. Blend in orange juice and vanilla. Add in powdered sugar and flour, beat until mixture thickens. Pour into a large bowl.

2. Clean mixer and beaters. Beat egg whites and cream of tarter until soft peaks form. Add sugar until you have stiff peaks.

3. Incorporate yolk mixture into egg white mixture until blended. Line two 8- inch round cake pans with parchment paper. Divide batter between the pans. Bake in a 325°F (170°C) oven for about 25 minutes, or until cake springs back when touched in the middle. Cool for 20 minutes. Run a spatula along rim of pan and invert cake onto a cooling rack. Peel off parchment paper. Cool completely. Frost with creamsicle frosting, or desired frosting. Serve with berries if desired.

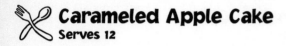

Carameled Apple Cake
Serves 12

This moist cake is delicious with or without the caramel frosting.

CAKE:

5 medium apples

2 sticks butter

1 cup (220 grams) brown sugar

⅔ cup (140 grams) white sugar

4 eggs

2⅔ cups (330 grams) rice flour

1 tablespoon baking powder

1 teaspoon cinnamon

½ teaspoon ground ginger

1½ cups (225 grams) raisins (optional)

CARAMEL:

10 teaspoons butter

4 tablespoons brown sugar

1 14-ounce (400-gram) can condensed milk

1. Coarsely grate the apples and set aside.

2. In a mixer cream together the butter and the sugars. Blend in the eggs. Add the flour, baking powder, cinnamon, and ginger. Mix until batter is smooth. Remove from mixer and stir in, by hand, the apples and raisins.

TRY MAKING the caramel sauce and dipping apple wedges in it for a quick dessert.

3. Pour into a parchment lined 13-inch × 9-inch baking pan. Bake in a 350°F (180°C) oven for 35 minutes. Set aside to cool.

4. For caramel, place the butter, sugar, and condensed milk in a saucepan and cook over medium-low heat, stirring constantly, until the mixture comes to a boil. Reduce the heat and cook for 5 minutes until the caramel is pale and thick. Remove from heat and set aside.

5. Invert cooled cake onto a baking tray and gently remove the parchment paper.

6. Pour caramel sauce over cake and gently help spread the caramel with a spatula over the top of the cake. Let cool completely and cut into bars.

Dairy-Free Variation: *Use oil or margarine in place of butter. Omit caramel sauce. Melt 1 stick margarine with ½ cup (110 grams) brown sugar and drizzle over cake.*

Egg-Free Variation: *Omit eggs and use ½ cup (125 grams) applesauce.*

Low-Sugar Variation: *Omit all sugars and add ½ cup (170 grams) Whey Low. Omit frosting.*

# Doughnut Cake
Serves 15

You can use this in place of shortcakes or pound cake. Sliced in thin layers and covered with chocolate frosting makes this my teenage brother's favorite cake. This recipe was also featured on glutenfree.com.

1½ cups (375 grams) butter

8 ounces (225 grams) cream cheese

2½ cups (500 grams) sugar

6 eggs

2 teaspoons powdered vanilla

3 cups (375 grams) rice flour

1 teaspoon salt

1. In a mixer with the paddle attachment beat the butter and cream cheese on low speed until smooth. Add the sugar and whip for 4 minutes. Add the eggs, vanilla, salt, and flour. Beat on low until smooth.

2. Grease a 10-inch tube pan lined with tinfoil, two 8-inch cake pans, or a large loaf pan. Pour batter into pan. Bake in a 325°F (170°C) oven for 1 hour (35 minutes for cake pans) or until cake is firm and golden. Remove and cool, about 1 hour. Remove from pan and peel off tinfoil. Let cool completely to room temperature. Slice and serve with cream and berries for a shortcake desert, or top with a chocolate glaze for a taste that is incredibly close to an Entenmanns' doughnut.

Dairy-Free Variation: *Substitute equal amounts of soy cream cheese for the cream cheese, and use stick margarine instead of butter.*

Low-Sugar Variation: *Use Whey Low.*

PART OF THE FUN of eating is cooking. Bring your children (assuming they are old enough) into the kitchen with you and teach them the culinary arts. I always include my little girls in the baking process. The toddler pulls the plastic containers and spoons from the cupboard, the preschooler likes to stir and scoop, and the oldest assists by cracking eggs and putting away the ingredients. It is fun for the little helpers to have a few ingredients in their own bowls. Have them mimic you cooking or let them be the head chef. My co-author likes to make a game of cooking with her children by having the children sing the names of the ingredients and then dance in the kitchen after the cake is in the oven. Make your own tradition in the kitchen, because, after all, home and hearth: they're the best of life, really!

Cocoa Pear Tart
Serves 6

This yummy morning treat has a festive flair; serve it during the holiday season to your children.

1 14-ounce (400-gram) can pear halves, drained
4 tablespoons butter
¼ cup (100 grams) sugar
2 eggs
1 cup (150 grams) almonds
2 tablespoons cocoa powder

1. In a food processor finely grind the almonds. Set aside
2. In a mixer, cream together butter and sugar until light and fluffy. Add the eggs and beat 1 minute more. Add the almonds and cocoa powder and blend on low speed until combined.
3. Butter an 8-inch glass tart pan. Pour the chocolate mixture in and press the pears on top, in a circle. Bake in a 400°F (200°C) oven for 25 minutes or until the filling has risen. Cool slightly and serve warm or cold.

Dairy-Free Variation: Use margarine or oil; use Nestlé cocoa powder.

Egg-Free Variation: Use 2 eggs' worth of Ener-G Egg Replacer and water.

Nut-Free Variation: Omit almond.

Lemon Raspberry Cheesecake
Serves 12

Made with very little sugar, everyone thinks this is the greatest. Be prepared to pass along this recipe!

2 tablespoons cookie crumbs, finely ground

16 ounces (455 grams) cottage cheese

16 ounces (455 grams) cream cheese

16 ounces (455 grams) sour cream

½ cup butter, melted

2 tablespoons lemon or orange juice

1 teaspoon powdered vanilla

½ cup (100 grams) sugar

4 tablespoons cornstarch

1 teaspoon grated lemon peel (optional)

4 eggs

1. In an 8- to 11-inch springform pan, butter the sides and bottom well. Add the 2 tablespoons of finely grated cookie crumbs and shake pan to coat sides and bottom. Flip upside down to discard excess crumbs.

2. In a blender or a food processor, blend the cottage cheese and the cream cheese together until smooth. Add the remaining ingredients. Blend until creamy with no lumps. Pour blended mixture into pan. Bake in a 350°F (180°C) oven for 1 hour and 15 minutes. Turn oven off and let sit in oven for 1 hour. Remove and let cool to room temperature. Cover and place in the refrigerator.

Dairy-Free and Egg-Free Variation: *Try Vegan Creamcake (see page 194).*

Low-Sugar Variation: *Replace with ½ cup Whey Low.*

MOST PEOPLE are familiar with the red variety of raspberries, but there are also black and white raspberries. Raspberries come from a rambling vine and prefer growing in cooler climates. Use fresh raspberries as soon as possible after purchasing as they tend to get moldy quickly.

Lemon Raspberry Topping
Makes 2 cups (420 grams)

This is a great sauce used in layers of cake or over ice cream.

12 ounces (340 grams) frozen raspberries (or blueberries), thawed

¼ cup (50 grams) sugar or concentrated raspberry juice

2 tablespoons juice or water

¼ cup (30 grams) cornstarch

1 teaspoon grated lemon peel

6 ounces (170 grams) white or semi-sweet chocolate

1. In a saucepan add the thawed raspberries and sugar or juice. Heat on low until raspberries begin to fall apart. Mix 2 tablespoons of juice or water with cornstarch. Add mixture to raspberries and turn up the heat to medium, stirring constantly until mixture thickens. Stir in lemon peel and set aside to cool.

2. Remove cheesecake from refrigerator. Uncover and pour warm raspberry mixture over entire surface of cheesecake. Re-cover and place back in refrigerator for 6 hours, or up to 48 hours. Remove when set. Melt chocolate in the microwave according to package directions. Pour into a sturdy zipper-lock bag. Cut a small tip off end and create your own unique design over the top of the cake. Run a knife around the rim of the pan and remove rim. Serve. Refrigerate leftovers, if there are any.

Low-Sugar Variation: Replace with Whey Low and omit chocolate.

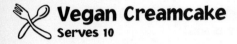

Vegan Creamcake
Serves 10

This is your basic dairy-free, egg-free cheesecake. When served with chocolate or fruit, it is even more delicious.

2½ cups (210 grams) gluten-free rice bran cookie
   crumbs (or homemade dairy-free brown
   sugar cookies)

½ cup (125 grams) margarine, melted

1 cup (230 grams) soy cream cheese

½ cup soy milk, mocha mix, or almond milk

¾ cup (90 grams) powdered sugar

1 teaspoon powdered vanilla

2 cups (400 grams) desired sliced fruits

¼ cup (80 grams) apricot preserves, melted

1. For the crust blend together the crumbs and the margarine. Press into a 10-inch glass pie pan or a springform pan. Bake in a 350°F (180°C) oven for 8 minutes. Set aside.

2. In a food processor or blender add the soy cream cheese, soy milk, powdered sugar, and vanilla. Blend until smooth. Pour into prepared pan. Refrigerate for 2 hours. Arrange fruits in a circular pattern. Brush on warm preserves over fruit. Chill and serve.

Variation: Blend ⅔ cup (120 grams) melted chocolate into the cream mixture.

Low-Sugar Variation: Use Whey Low. Omit preserves.

HAVING A BIRTHDAY PARTY? Try this Star Cake. Make the cake in two 8-inch round cake pans and fill with a fruit filling. Frost with a white frosting. Make a recipe of Fun Cut-Outs dough. Using biscuit cutters, cut out into desired shapes (stars, baseballs and bats, soccer balls, ballet slippers, etc.). Bake and decorate the cookies. Push cookies around into the frosted cake. Place a few cookies on top of the cake with the child's name on one cookie and "Happy Birthday" on another. Decorate borders with colored sugar or additional frosting. Decorate remaining cookies and send them home as gifts!

Yellow Cake
Serves 12

This is your basic "box" cake recipe. Use it for whatever you need.

3 eggs
1½ cups (300 grams) sugar
2 teaspoons powdered vanilla
2 sticks butter, chilled
3 cups (375 grams) rice flour
2 teaspoons baking powder
1 teaspoon baking soda
½ teaspoon salt
1½ cups buttermilk

1. In a mixer with the paddle attachment whip the eggs and sugar until light and fluffy, about 3 minutes. Add the vanilla. Cut the butter into thin slices and add it to the mixture; beat on high for an additional 3 minutes.

2. Add the flour, baking powder, baking soda, and salt. Stir on low until combined. With mixer on low, slowly add the buttermilk until well combined.

3. Pour into two 8-inch parchment-lined cake pans. Bake in a 350°F (180°C) oven for 35 minutes or until lightly browned and firm in the center.

4. Let cool. Invert onto a cooling rack. Frost with desired frosting. Whipped cream and berries go nicely.

Egg-Free Variation: Use 3 eggs' worth of Ener-G Egg Replacer.

Dairy-Free Variation: Replace buttermilk with ¾ cup soy yogurt, ¾ cup rice milk, and 1 ½ Tablespoons lemon juice. Replace butter with margarine.

Low-Sugar Variation: Use Whey Low.

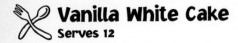

Vanilla White Cake
Serves 12

This is a perfect birthday cake recipe. Frost with any desired frosting.

5 eggs, separated

½ cup (100 grams) sugar

½ cup milk

1 4-ounce (115-gram) package vanilla instant pudding

1¼ cups (155 grams) white rice flour

2 teaspoons powdered vanilla

1. In a mixer beat the egg yolks until pale yellow; add the sugar, milk, pudding, flour, and vanilla. Beat until thick. Pour into a bowl and set aside.

2. In a clean mixer bowl, beat egg whites until stiff peaks form. Fold in the vanilla-egg mixture.

3. Pour into two 8-inch parchment-lined cake pans. Bake in a 325°F (170°C) oven for 35 minutes. Let cool. Invert onto a cooling rack and gently peel off the parchment. Cool completely before frosting.

Dairy-Free Variation: *Follow recipe for Yellow Cake, page 195.*

Egg-Free Variation: *Omit eggs. Before creaming sugar, mix together 5 teaspoons of Ener-G Egg Replacer with 5 tablespoons of water and add. Continue with recipe, except omit the egg white stage.*

ONE OF THE HARDEST parts of being a kid with a wheat allergy is never getting to eat the cupcakes brought for all the birthdays in elementary schools. Even worse, perhaps, is when your birthday falls during the school year, and you can't eat a cupcake, so you don't bring them. Now you can. Make up a batch of these for everyone! Your child will enjoy celebrating with all the other kids and the other kids will love this wheat-free rendition of the old standby.

COOKING CAN actually turn into a mathematics lesson. Whenever you use measuring cups, explain to your children the fractions of the whole. Your child will soon remember, for example, that four ¼ cups make 1 whole cup.

Wonder Cake
Serves 12

This cake is basically free of all allergens. It is, indeed, a wonder. It is perfectly full of taste and tenderness. For those with chocolate intolerances, remember the fruit-based cakes. There truly is something for everyone!

1 teaspoon egg replacer plus 2 tablespoons water

⅓ cup (115 grams) each honey and molasses

6 tablespoons olive oil

1¾ cups (215 grams) rice flour

Dash of salt

2 teaspoons cinnamon

2 teaspoons baking powder

½ teaspoon baking soda

1 cup apple juice

1 small apple, chopped

1 small pear, chopped

½ cup (75 grams) raisins

1. Cream together the egg replacer and the water. Blend the honey, molasses, and oil. Add the flour, salt, cinnamon, baking powder, and soda. On low speed mix in the juice. Stir in the chopped apple, pear, and raisins.

2. Pour into a parchment-lined 8- or 9-inch cake pan. Bake in a 350°F (180°C) oven for 45 minutes.

Low-Sugar Variation: Omit honey and molasses.

My Size Pies
Serves about 12

Take your pick of which fabulous filling you want. These are the perfect treat for little hands. Use your favorite tapioca-based fruit pie recipe in this too. Just cook it over the stovetop and pour into prebaked pie crusts.

3 cups milk

½ cup (100 grams) sugar

8 tablespoons cornstarch

3 eggs (reserve 2 egg whites for meringues)

1 tablespoon butter

2 tablespoons powdered vanilla

1 recipe of any pie crust or cookie crust, chilled

1. In a medium saucepan combine the milk, sugar, and the cornstarch. Stir over medium heat until comes to a thick roll. Remove from heat. In a bowl whisk 1 whole egg and 2 egg yolks together. Whisk 1 tablespoon of milk mixture into egg mixture. Repeat with 1 tablespoon at a time until egg mixture is warm. Stir egg mixture into milk mixture and return to a medium heat; cook while constantly stirring for 4 minutes. Remove from heat and stir in butter and vanilla. Set aside.

2. Roll 12 balls of dough using 2 tablespoons of dough each. Grease a muffin tin. Push each dough ball into bottom and sides of muffin tin. Use plastic wrap and added rice flour to help dough not stick to hands, or wet your hands and pat in. Bake in a 350°F (180°C) oven for 15 minutes.

 MY SIZE PIE VARIATIONS:

Chocolate pies, add 1 cup (135 grams) semisweet chocolate chips to the milk mixture.

Coconut pies, add 1 cup (70 grams) shredded coconut after adding the butter.

Banana pies, add 1 banana sliced small after adding the butter.

Butterscotch, add brown sugar in place of sugar.

Pudding cups, omit crust and place into desired amount of cups.

Fruit pies, follow the pie directions on the back of a tapioca box!

3. Re-stir pudding mixture and fill each muffin tin. Refrigerate for 2 hours, covered.

4. With reserved egg white mixture, make a recipe for Meringue Shapes (sidebar page 156). Pipe meringue into 3-dimensional stars or clouds that would fit on each mini pie. Let meringue shape cool completely before placing on pies. Decorate with added melted chocolate, if desired.

Dairy-Free Variation: *Increase cornstarch to ⅓ cup (40 grams) and use desired milk substitute such as Soy, Almond, Mocha Mix, etc. Replace butter with margarine.*

Egg-Free Variation: *Omit eggs and meringue tops. Use whipped cream or nondairy whipped topping for tops.*

Low-Sugar Variation: *Use Whey Low.*

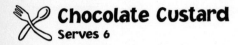 # Chocolate Custard
Serves 6

1½ cups milk (1 can evaporated milk)

⅓ cup (70 grams) sugar

1 cup (175 grams) semisweet chocolate chips

3 eggs, beaten

1. In a saucepan combine the milk, sugar, and the chocolate chips. Cook over medium heat and stir until smooth. Slowly whisk the beaten egg into chocolate mixture in a steady stream while constantly stirring. Pour mixture into four ramekins or an 8-inch glass custard dish. Place dish in a large baking pan and fill with water a quarter of the way up. Bake in a 325°F (170°C) oven for 30 minutes or until set in the center. Serve warm or chilled.

Dairy-Free Variation: Use 1¼ cups of soy or almond milk, and Ener-G semisweet chocolate.

Egg-Free Variation: Use 3 eggs' worth of Ener-G Egg Replacer mixed with directed amount of water. Cream together before adding to chocolate mixture.

Low-Sugar Variation: Replace with Whey Low.

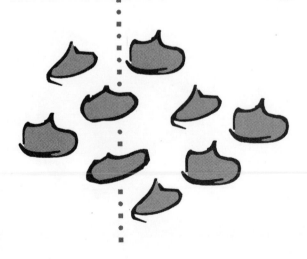

Blueberry Custard
Serves 6

1 cup cream

2 egg yolks

¼ cup (50 grams) sugar

½ cup (125 grams) butter, melted

1 cup (145 grams) blueberries

1. Mix the cream, egg yolks, sugar, and butter.
2. In a glass 8-inch round baking pan, place the blueberries over the bottom. Pour the cream mixture over.
3. Bake in a 350°F (180°C) oven for 60 minutes.

Dairy-Free Variation: *Omit cream and butter; use 1 cup coconut milk and ½ cup (125 grams) margarine.*

Egg-Free Variation: *Follow the recipe for Chocolate Custard (facing page), replacing chocolate chips with 1 cup blueberries.*

Low-Sugar Variation: *Replace with Whey Low.*

Store-Bought Chocolate Cake
Serves about 20

This recipe is so versatile! It can make two 8-inch cakes, 24 cupcakes, or a 9-inch plate of brownies. You will be amazed at how tasty and easy it is to make this cake.

2 cups (250 grams) rice flour

⅔ cup water or milk

2 cups (400 grams) sugar

2 sticks (1 cup) butter or oil

½ teaspoon salt

2 cups (350 grams) semisweet chocolate chips

6 eggs

1 teaspoon vanilla

1. In a saucepan over medium heat, stir together the water, butter, and sugar. Bring to a boil, stirring constantly. Remove from heat and stir in the chocolate chips until smooth.

2. Stir in the flour. Working quickly, stir in the eggs. Stir in remaining ingredients.

3. Line your cake pans with tinfoil or parchment paper. Pour in batter. Bake in a 350°F (180°C) oven. Cupcakes bake for 10 minutes, cake pans bake for 16 minutes, and a brownie pan bakes for 15 minutes. Let cool completely, peel off foil, and frost.

Variation: After pouring batter in cake pans, sprinkle in 1 cup (175 grams) of your favorite chocolate chips. I like adding mint chips. Mini M&M's taste good, too!

Dairy-Free Variation: Replace milk with water, and butter with oil; use Ener-G chocolate chips.

Egg-Free Variation: Use 6 eggs' worth of Ener-G Egg Replacer.

DO THE KIDS WANT Hostess Cupcakes? Try making these cupcakes and filling them with Marshmallow Cream. Simply cut out cylinders from each cupcake and fill with cream. Cut off tips of the cylinder and place over the cream. Frost with chocolate ganache or frosting. With white frosting make zigzags across top. Yum!

✗ The Perfect Pie Crust
Serves 6

I prefer this crust for all my fruit pies and my quiches.

¾ cup (90 grams) rice flour

1½ cups (150 grams) oat meal or rice bran

¼ teaspoon salt

¼ cup oil

1 egg

3 tablespoons corn syrup, honey, or maple syrup

2 teaspoons water (optional)

1. In a food processor add the flour and oatmeal. Pulse until you have a blended flour.

2. Add the remaining ingredients. Pulse until you have a firm dough that forms a ball. If mixture does not form into a ball add water one teaspoon at a time.

3. Roll between two pieces of plastic wrap. Lift up one piece of wrap and place dough-side down on a pie plate. Pat dough firmly into pie plate. Lift up remaining piece of wrap. Pour in desired filling and bake as usual.

Variation: Roll dough flat onto a baking tray. Sprinkle with coarse salt. Prick several times with a fork. Bake at 350°F (180°C) for 8 minutes. Cut into squares. You have just made the yummiest wheat-free, thin crackers.

Egg-Free Variation: Use 1 egg's worth of Ener-G Egg Replacer.

Low-Sugar Variation: Use sugar-free maple syrup.

Cream Cheese Push-in Crust
Serves 6

This crust is very tasty and easy. Just pat it into whatever size pie pans you are using. This works well for sweet or savory.

2 cups (250 grams) white rice flour

½ cup (125 grams) butter, cut into pieces

½ cup (115 grams) cream cheese

½ cup (60 grams) cornstarch

1 teaspoon salt

4 tablespoons sugar

3 eggs

3 tablespoons cold water

1. In a food processor add the flour, butter, and cream cheese. Pulse until it resembles pea-size pieces. Add the cornstarch, salt, and sugar. Pulse for 30 seconds. Add eggs one at a time while processor is on, only until dough starts to form into a ball. Add water if needed. To test this, turn processor off and pinch off a bit of dough. The dough should easily roll into a ball in your hands without being too sticky. If too sticky, add a handful of flour, pulse, and repeat process. If dough seems dry, add water a little at a time.

Dairy-Free Variation: Use margarine and soy cream cheese in place of butter and cream cheese.

Egg-Free Variation: Use 3 eggs' worth of Ener-G Egg Replacer.

Low-Sugar Variation: Use Whey Low.

WANT TO DECORATE your cakes, cookies, and cupcakes? Chocolate to the rescue! Melt your choice of chocolate chips, place in a zipper-lock bag with the tip cut off, and pipe out zigzags, letters, and stripes. Or melt together 6 ounces of semisweet chocolate and 1 tablespoon of shortening. Place in a bag and pipe out shapes like stars or hearts on a lined baking tray. Place in the freezer for 15 minutes, peel chocolate off tinfoil, and stick on your cakes for a bakery-style dessert everyone will rave over.

Candy Bar Chocolate Frosting
Makes enough for 1 cake

This frosting takes a little time but it is definitely worth it! My mother-in-law likes when I make it for her. She keeps it in the freezer and eats it with a spoon!

1¼ cups cream

¼ cup (85 grams) light corn syrup

¼ cup (60 grams) butter

1 16-ounce (455-gram) package milk
    chocolate, chopped

1. In a saucepan combine the cream, corn syrup, and butter. Whisk mixture until it begins to simmer over medium heat. Add the chocolate. Reduce heat to low and continue stirring until melted and smooth.

2. In a mixer, with the whisk, pour the hot chocolate mixture in and beat for 10 minutes until mixture cools and becomes lighter in color. Frosting is ready when it forms soft peaks.

3. For a chocolate glaze, decrease cream to 1 cup, corn syrup to 2 tablespoons, and omit butter. Add 1½ cups (265 grams) milk chocolate or semi-sweet chocolate. Follow directions for step 1. Cool until thickened. Use this to glaze Doughnut Cake or to dip cookies into. Let chocolate glaze cool completely on cake or cookies before serving.

Dairy-Free Variation: Try Dairy-Free Frosting (see page 207) made with Nestlé cocoa powder.

Creamsicle Frosting
Makes enough for 1 cake

8 ounces (225 grams) cream cheese

½ cup (125 grams) butter

2 cups (240 grams) powdered sugar

3 tablespoons frozen orange juice concentrate, thawed

2 teaspoons powdered vanilla

1. In a mixer fitted with a paddle attachment, whip cream cheese and butter until fluffy. Add the powdered sugar and orange juice. Blend well. Add the vanilla and whip for 20 more seconds. Spread onto muffins, cupcakes, or frost 1 two-layer cake.

Dairy-Free Variation: Use soy cream cheese and margarine.
Low-Sugar Variation: Replace sugar with 1 cup Whey Low and 2 tsp cornstarch.

Cinnamon Sweet Frosting
Makes enough for 1 cake

2 8-ounce (225-gram) packages cream cheese

½ cup (125 grams) butter

½ cup (110 grams) brown sugar

½ cup (60 grams) powdered sugar

½ teaspoon ground cinnamon

½ teaspoon ground ginger

1 teaspoon powdered vanilla

1. In a food processor, combine the cream cheese and butter; blend until smooth. Add remaining ingredients and pulse on and off until smooth. Spread on the cake. Or microwave a few seconds until soft and use on your Bundt cakes.

Dairy-Free Variation: Use soy cream cheese and margarine.

ALTHOUGH NOT EDIBLE, you can find really interesting cake decorations at the fabric store. Use your imagination and use bows and strings of beads to decorate your culinary creations. For birthdays, I tie large ribbons around my cakes and cheesecakes; everyone thinks they're the greatest gifts.

Royal Icing
Makes about 1 cup (180 grams)

This dries quickly and has a beautiful, shiny appearance. Perfect for decorative cookies and detailed decorations on cakes.

1 tablespoon powdered egg whites
1⅓ cups (160 grams) powdered sugar
2 tablespoons water

1. In a mixer add all ingredients. Beat together until the consistency of glue. If desired, add 1 teaspoon powdered vanilla.
2. You may thin with 1 to 3 teaspoons of corn syrup for drizzling over desserts or dipping cookies in. Divide in portions and tint with different colors if desired.

Low-Sugar Variation: Use Whey Low.

Dairy-Free Frosting
Makes enough for 1 cake

½ cup (125 grams) margarine
½ cup (125 grams) shortening
4 cups (480 grams) powdered sugar
4 teaspoons powdered vanilla

1. In a mixer with a paddle attachment whip the margarine and shortening together until fluffy. Add the sugar and vanilla; whip until smooth. Frost cookies, cupcakes, or 1 two-layer cake.

Variation: Add ¼ cup (45 grams) melted Ener-G semisweet chocolate after the sugar and vanilla. Or use 2 tablespoons of Nestlé cocoa. For a glaze, add 2 tablespoons of lemon juice. Use over a Bundt cake or for cookies.

Low-Sugar Variation: Use Whey Low.

Marshmallow Frosting
Makes enough for 1 cake

2 egg whites

Dash salt

¾ cup (255 grams) light corn syrup

2 teaspoons powdered vanilla

1. In a mixer with the paddle attachment, beat the egg whites and salt until very white and fluffy.
2. Meanwhile, heat the syrup in a saucepan over medium heat until boiling.
3. With mixer on medium speed, add the syrup to the egg whites in a steady thin stream. Add the vanilla and return the mixer to high speed and beat until fluffy and easy to spread.

Egg-Free Variation: Try Dairy-Free Frosting (see page 207).

Honey Cream Frosting
Makes enough for 1 cake

This is not an overly sweet frosting and it is great on any cake or muffin containing fruit.

8 ounces (225 grams) cream cheese or soy cream cheese

¼ cup (60 grams) firm honey (not runny)

1. In a mixer with the paddle attachment, beat cream cheese on medium speed until fluffy, about 2 minutes. Add honey and beat until smooth.

Homemade Marshmallows
Serves 16

1½ cups water, divided

4 envelopes unflavored gelatin

3 cups (600 grams) sugar

1¼ cups (425 grams) light corn syrup

¼ teaspoon salt

2½ teaspoons powdered vanilla

1 cup (120 grams) powdered sugar

1. Pour ¾ cup water in the bowl of a mixer. Sprinkle with gelatin; let soften for 5 minutes.

2. Place the sugar, corn syrup, salt, and an additional ¾ cup water in a saucepan and bring to a boil about 4 minutes (a candy thermometer should register 240°F or 116°C).

3. With the mixer on low speed, carefully add hot syrup to the gelatin mixture, pouring in a long, thin stream. Increase speed to high and beat until stiff peaks form, about 28 minutes. Beat in the vanilla.

4. Pour mixture into a greased 9-inch × 13-inch glass baking dish. Let stand at room temperature for 5 hours until firm. Sift powdered sugar onto baking tray lined with tinfoil. Invert pan onto baking tray. Using an oiled knife, cut into desired size squares. Roll in powdered sugar.

Hershey's Milk-Free Dark Bark
Makes about 2 cups (360 grams)

1 8-ounce (225-gram) package Hershey's Unsweetened
  Baking Chocolate, broken into pieces

¼ cup (60 grams) plus 1 teaspoon shortening

⅛ teaspoon powdered vanilla

2 cups (240 grams) confectioners' sugar

1. In a medium bowl, microwave chocolate and shortening on high for 1½ to 2 minutes, until mixture is melted and smooth when stirred.

2. Add powdered vanilla.

3. Gradually stir in confectioners' sugar. If mixture becomes too thick, knead with clean hands.

4. Spread out in pan.

5. Cover tightly; refrigerate until firm.

6. Break into pieces.

7. Store well covered, in refrigerator.

Low-Sugar Variation: Use 2 cups Whey Low.

LOVE CHOCOLATE? And who makes the most famous chocolates in America? Hershey's. Chances are you've baked with plenty of Hershey's chocolates. To make sure that any Hershey's products you use are gluten-free, just call the company at 1-800-468-1714, 9–4 EST. For fun information about the new products and offers, surf to their site at www.hersheys.com.

Fancy Fruit
Serves 6

This is a fabulous dessert idea. Make it as simple or as fancy as you want. Try bringing this to a child's classroom party—it is a guaranteed hit!

15 strawberries

1 cup (175 grams) chocolate, melted (milk, semisweet, and white chocolate work great)

Sweets, colored sugar, or sprinkles

1. Wash and dry the strawberries. Keep the stems on.

2. Melt chocolate according to package directions. Pour into a heavy-duty zipper-lock bag. Cut a small tip off one side. Zigzag strips of chocolate over each piece of fruit. Or pour melted chocolate into a bowl and dip each strawberry halfway in. Place on a wax paper-lined baking tray. Sprinkle with sweets or sprinkles. You may use a variety of different chocolates to decorate with. Be creative. Refrigerate until ready to use. Remove fruit from wax paper and place on a serving plate.

Variation: Fresh pineapple spears and apple slices are also good. Make sure they are washed and dried really well.

Ice Cream Bowls
Serves 6

Use instead of cones for ice cream and frozen yogurt.
Fresh fruit and whipped cream make a great treat, too!

1 egg white

4 tablespoons sugar

1½ tablespoons rice flour

1 teaspoon cornstarch

2 tablespoons Nestlé cocoa powder

2 tablespoons melted butter

1. Beat the egg white and sugar until soft peaks form.
2. Fold in the flour, cornstarch, cocoa, and butter.
3. Line a baking tray with parchment paper. Spread out 1 table-spoon of mixture to a 5-inch circle.
4. Bake in a 400°F (200°C) oven for 4–5 minutes. Remove and immediately mold over an upturned glass cup or a muffin tin. Let cool for 10 minutes.

Dairy-Free Variation: *Replace butter with margarine.*

Low-Sugar Variation: *Use Whey Low.*

ANOTHER CHOCOLATE bowl idea is to turn a muffin tin over and coat with cooking spray. Drizzle melted semisweet chocolate over the tin back and forth and coat bottom well. Freeze for 15 minutes and then pop the chocolate bowl off the muffin tin. Fill with ice cream and serve immediately. You can place the ready-made ice cream-filled bowls in the freezer until ready to serve, if desired. These make great party desserts.

Cream Puffs
Serves 12

These are fabulous because no one can tell they are wheat-free! Fill with desired fillings. One year I tinted the dough orange, made the puffs, filled them with pumpkin pudding, and decorated the tops like green leaves to make the most adorable edible pumpkins you have ever seen!

1 cup water

½ cup (125 grams) butter

1 teaspoon sugar

½ teaspoon salt

2 cups (250 grams) rice flour

5 eggs

1. In a saucepan combine water, butter, sugar, and salt. Bring to a boil. Immediately stir in the flour. Return to heat and stir constantly to dry out the dough a bit, for about 3 minutes.

2. Transfer the dough to your mixer. With your paddle attachment, mix on low speed to cool the dough for about 2 minutes. Add the eggs one at a time until smooth.

3. Push the dough into a large zipper-lock bag with the tip cut off or a pastry bag. On a parchment- or tinfoil-lined baking tray, pipe out 2- to 4-inch balls.

4. Place into a 425°F (220°C) oven to puff the dough for about 10 minutes. Turn the heat down to 350°F (180°C) and bake an additional 15 minutes.

   Remove from oven to a cooling rack. Repeat heating directions with remaining dough.

5. To fill, you may poke a hole in the bottom of the puff. Use desired filling in a plastic bag or a pastry bag. Sprinkle with powdered sugar or drizzle with chocolate.

Dairy-Free Variation: *Replace butter with margarine.*

Low-Sugar Variation: *Omit sugar.*

Flourless Gourmet Brownies
Serves 10

This fabulous dessert is worthy of pleasing the most demanding child as well as on the table at the most elegant dinner party!

6 eggs

¾ cup (150 grams) sugar

1½ sticks butter

2 cups (350 grams) semisweet chocolate chips

3 teaspoons vanilla

1. In a mixer with the paddle attachment, whip eggs and sugar on high for 5 minutes until thick and light in color.

2. Meanwhile, in a microwave-proof bowl, combine the butter and chocolate chips and microwave at 30-second intervals until chocolate becomes soft and butter melts. Stir until smooth. Let cool slightly. Stir in vanilla.

3. Pour ½ cup chocolate mixture into egg mixture and stir rapidly. Add the remaining chocolate mixture and stir until well combined.

4. Line a 9-inch square baking pan with tinfoil or parchment paper. Pour mixture in and place in a 350°F (180°C) oven for about 1 hour. Remove and let cool completely. For best results, refrigerate overnight. When firm, invert onto a cutting board, peel off tinfoil, and cut into small squares. Keep chilled.

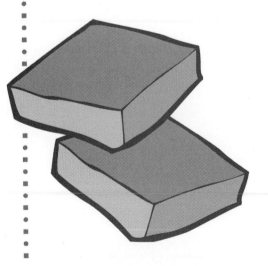

Variation: Add an additional cup of chocolate chips—mint chips are yummy—to the mixture before pouring into a baking pan.

Dairy-Free Variation: Replace butter with margarine. Use Ener-G chocolate chips

Egg-Free Variation: Try Store-Bought Chocolate Cake (see page 202).

# Low-Sugar Blintzes
Serves 8

These are a delicious treat. Replace the honey with maple syrup or powdered sugar if you like.

CREPES:

1 cup milk or soy milk

2 eggs

1 cup (125 grams) rice flour

1½ tablespoons olive oil

FILLING:

1 cup (225 grams) cottage cheese

2 ounces (55 grams) cream cheese

1 teaspoon vanilla

1 tablespoon honey

1. In a bowl mix milk, eggs, flour, and oil until smooth.

2. Place a 7-inch frying pan (crepe pan) over medium-high heat until a drop of water immediately evaporates.

3. Ladle enough batter into pan while swirling the pan around to coat with a thin, even pancake. Cook for about a minute or until the pancake starts to curl on the sides. Flip and cook about 30 seconds more. Stack on a plate and cover.

4. For the filling, combine all ingredients in a food processor and blend until smooth.

5. To assemble, fill a crepe with about 3 tablespoons of cream filling. Fold two sides in. Roll opposite side over to seam. Place seam-side down. Top with fresh fruit, applesauce, or whipped cream, and serve.

Dairy-Free Variation: Fill with 1 cup soy yogurt and ¼ cup sliced fruit.

Egg-Free Variation: Omit eggs and use 2 eggs' worth of Ener-G Egg Replacer and water.

Low-Sugar Variation: Omit honey.

HELPFUL HINTS

Here are some helpful tips to keep kids feeling more included during parties and school activities. Most art materials like play dough and paints are made from potential irritants from dairy, peanut, or gluten. You can go online to www.nickelodeon.com for fun slime and dough ideas, just make sure to use the cornstarch-based recipes. Remember, just because your child has food restrictions does not mean she can't have a fun birthday party!

The Princess Dream Party

Make a variety of delicate snacks, including:

Fruit and Marshmallow Sauce (see page 28)
On the Trail Mix (see page 28)
Devilish Eggs (see page 45)
Mini Quiches (see page 71)
Jumbo Vanilla Cherry Muffins with Chocolate
    Chips—just make them mini (see page 84)

Serve with Lemonade or the Horchata Rice drink
(see page 24).

For dessert:
Barbie Doll Cake
Serves 20-30 (small slices)

Vanilla White Cake (see page 196; double the
    recipe for two cakes)
4 containers of gluten-free purchased vanilla
    frosting, or homemade dairy-free vanilla frosting
    (see page 207; quadruple the recipe if you
    choose to make your own)

1. Combine ingredients for Vanilla White Cake and
   pour into two tinfoil-lined bundt pans.

2. Bake at directed temperature for 60 minutes, or until
   the cake springs back at the center (this may require
   more time if you bake both at once). Let cool for 20
   minutes. Invert onto a cooling rack and peel off foil.

3. Turn one cake bottom-side up, and push a Dixie
   cup into the bottom.

4. Frost, and then place the second cake bottom
   side down. Push a new Barbie doll into the center
   of the cake. Lift her arms and tie up her hair.
   Frost her entire dress (the cake) and tint remaining frosting with desired colors. Then place this
   remaining, colored frosting in a pastry bag or
   ziplock bag with the corner cut off, and use that
   to decorate the cake. You may follow the pattern
   of a Princess Barbie box, or consult a cake deco-
   rating book. Sprinkle Barbie with colored sugar,
   or use sugared roses. Place a decorated, large
   marshmallow in her hands for a cute present.

The Little Slugger's Party

Make a variety of yummy snacks including:

Nacho Quesadillas cut out into star and
    baseball shapes (see page 69)
Spinach Dip with carrots and potato crisps
    (see page 31)
Mock Goldfish Crackers (see page 44)
Baked Potato Nachos (see page 65)

Serve with homemade apple juice.

For dessert:
Stars and Baseballs Cake
Serves 20-30 (small slices)

2 cakes of any flavor you desire
4 containers of gluten-free purchased vanilla
    frosting, or homemade dairy-free vanilla
    frosting (see page 207; quadruple the ingredi-
    ents if you choose to make your own)

1. Follow the directions for baking two cakes from
   a recipe of your liking, using 8-9 inch round
   cake pans.

2. Cool for 20 minutes.

3. Place one cake down, frost, and then place the
   second cake on top. Frost the top and sides.

4. Make one recipe of Fun Cut-Out dough (see page
   166), or Easy Multi-Purpose Sugar Cookie Dough
   (see page 163). Roll out the dough, and use biscuit
   cutters to make star, baseball, and bat shapes.
   Soccer balls and footballs work well too.

5. Bake cookies and let cool. Frost with tinted colors
   like blue, red, green, and yellow. Within four
   hours of serving, place star cookies around sides
   of frosted cake. Place one baseball and one bat on
   top. Write the name of your child over the ball,
   and write "Happy Birthday" underneath. Frost
   the border of the cake and sprinkle it with colored
   sugar. Serve additional cookies on side.

Fiesta Party Pleasers
Serves 25
Especially suitable to a buffet or large crowd, there is something here to appeal to almost anyone's needs.

Make one recipe of each:
Tortilla Soup (see page 117)
Layered Vegetarian Enchilada (see page 129)
Corn Bread with Everything (see page 145)
Taco Salad (see page 136)
Green Chile Bean Bake (see page 149)

Serve with tortilla chips and salsa. For a very large crowd you can cut Mexican Pizzas into single servings. For dessert try the Chocolate Cake with Chocolate Frosting (see pages 184, 205) or Carrot Cupcakes with Cinnamon Sweet Frosting (see pages 186, 206).

Bunny Cake
Serves 20-30 (small slices)
Carrot Cake (see page 186)
2 cups (140 grams) coconut
1 container of gluten-free purchased vanilla frosting, or homemade dairy-free vanilla frosting (see page 207)
2 strawberries
assorted candies
food coloring

1. Bake cake according to instructions, remove from the oven and let cool.

2. Cut cake in half and frost the tops. Push together so cut surface is on the bottom (it should look like a rainbow).

3. Frost entire cake and cover with coconut. Use sweets to decorate the bunny face at one end of the "rainbow" and extra frosting and coconut to design ears and the bunny tail.

4. Cut two strawberries in half and place each half near the bottom, like bunny feet, large part in front, small part of strawberry pointing towards the tail. The cake should resemble a sitting bunny.

*Use same cake pattern and frost with primary colors to make a rainbow cake.

Clay Dough
Did you know that most play dough contains gluten? Wendy's school teacher invented this recipe for her. This dough dries nicely and is perfectly white. We paint our creations after they dry.

1 cup (125 grams) white rice flour
1 cup (292 grams) salt
¾ cup water

1. Mix all ingredients together in a bowl. Roll the dough into a firm ball. If the mixture is too crumbly, add additional water 1 teaspoon at a time.

2. Have children make snowmen, or use biscuit cutters to make shapes.

3. Line a baking tray with tinfoil and let dry completely, for at least 1 day.

4. If you'd like, you can bake the clay dough at 200°F (93°C) for about 30 minutes before painting.

Flexible Play Dough
You do have to cook this on the stove-top, but we find that it lasts well and is perfect to keep at school and use in the Play Dough Fun Centers.

1½ cup (180 grams) corn starch
½ cup (60 grams) rice flour
2 cup water
2 teaspoons cream of tartar
1 cup (292 grams) salt
1 tablespoon oil

1. Mix all ingredients in a sauce pan, and cook over medium heat, stirring constantly until the dough begins to solidify (this usually takes about 5 minutes).

2. Place in a large plastic bowl to cool. When dough is cool to the touch, divide into portions and place in a ziplock bag. Add desired amounts of food coloring to bag and seal. Have your child knead the bag until dough becomes evenly colored.

3. Store covered in the refrigerator for about a month. Bring to room temperature before using.

INDEX

—A—

Alfredo and Chives, 101

Allergies. See Food intolerances/allergies

Allergy and Asthma Network Literature, 92

Almonds
Cocoa Pear Tart, 191
Crinkle Crunchies, 168
Horchata Rice Drink, 24

Anaphylaxis, 38, 142

Antihistamines, 142

Apples
Apple Rice Pudding, 172
Brown Rice and Apple Salad, 53
Carameled Apple Cake, 188–89
health benefits of, 20–21, 22
Rainbow Happy Healthy Juice, 23

Applesauce
Applesauce Parfait, 22
Basic, 20
Blue, 21
Cinnamon, 22
Pink, 21

Asian dishes
Broccoli Beef Noodles, 130
Fried Rice, 151
Rice Pinwheels, 62–63
Rice Snowballs, 61
Spring Rolls, 60
Teriyaki Veggie Spears, 143
Thai Rolls, 59
Ubu, 64

Astor, Stephen, 90

Autism spectrum disorders, 64

Avocado
Guacamole Salsa, 66

Awesome Blueberries, 78

—B—

Baby Biscotti, 87

Baked Potato Nachos, 65

Baking powder, 17

Baking products, 16–17

Baking soda, 17, 186

Bananas
Banana Bread Muffins, 77
PB and Banana Chip Muffins, 80
pies, 198
Vegan Tropical Muffins, 85

Barbara's, 16

Barbie Doll Cake, 218

Bars. See Cookies and bars

Basic Applesauce, 20

Beans
Bean Dip, 32
Bean Salad, 47
Chili-Mac, 124
Good Morning Enchilada Strata, 96
Green Bean Bake, 148
Green Chili Bean Bake, 149
Hot Dog, Bean, and Tortilla Casserole, 134
Layered Vegetarian Enchiladas, 129
Mexican Five-Layer Dip, 33
Mexican Pizza, 68
Mexican-Style Baked Beans, 146
Nacho Quesadillas, 69
Polenta Snack Cakes, 76
Salsa Bean and Rice Salad, 54
Taco Salad Meal, 136
Tortilla Soup, 117
Vegetarian Tamale Casserole, 122

Beef
Broccoli Beef Noodles, 130
Chili-Mac, 124
Grandma's Tamale Casserole, 121
Happy Burgers, 139
Pastitsio, 102–3
Pizza Noodles, 116
Sloppy Joe Potato Skillet, 125
Taco Salad Meal, 136
Upside-Down Pizza, 113

Berries
See Blackberries, Blueberries, Raspberries, Strawberries

Beverages
Horchata Rice Drink, 24
Rainbow Happy Healthy Juice, 23

Birthday party ideas, 218–19

Biscotti, Baby, 87

Black beans. See Beans

Blackberries
Blue Pancake Crepes with Blue Applesauce and Honey Syrup, 91
Blue Applesauce, 21
Blue Pancake Crepes with Blue Applesauce and Honey Syrup, 91

Blueberries
Applesauce Parfait, 22
Awesome Blueberries (muffins), 78
Blue Applesauce, 21
Blue Pancake Crepes with Blue Applesauce and Honey Syrup, 91
Blueberry Custard, 201
Lemon Berry Bars, 170
Very Berry Muffins, 83

Bob's Red Mill, 14, 16

Braly, James, 37

Bran and Raisin Muffins, 82

Breads
Banana Bread, 77
Corn Bread with Everything, 145
Cut Out Croutons, 41
French Toast Bake, 94
Homemade Pizza Dough, 110
recommended brands, 14

Breakfast dishes
Blue Pancake Crepes with Blue Applesauce and Honey Syrup, 91
Breakfast Skillet, 95
Buttermilk Pancakes, 90
French Toast Bake, 94
Good Morning Enchilada Strata, 96
Pancake Torte, 93
Scrambled Egg Enchiladas, 97

Breastfeeding, 47, 132

Broccoli
Broccoli Beef Noodles, 130
Hot and Yummy Pockets, 70

Brown Rice and Apple Salad, 53

Brown Sugar Dough, 159

Brownies
Flourless Gourmet Brownies, 214
Frosted Brownies, 179

Buckwheat
about, 42
Chewy Granola Bars, 42
Crunchy Granola Bars, 37
Morning Bars, 43

Bunny Cake, 219

Butter, Whipped Fruit, 29

Buttermilk Pancakes, 90

Buttermilk substitute, 83

Butternut squash
Harvest Soup, 118
Risotto Parmesan Butternut Squash Bake, 104

Butterscotch Pies, 198

—C—

Cabbage
Rice Vinegar Asian Salad, 52
Spring Rolls, 60

Cake decorations, 207

Cakes See also Frostings
Barbie Doll Cake, 218
Bunny Cake, 219
Carameled Apple Cake, 188–89
Carrot Cake, 186
Chocolate Cake, 184–85
Creamsicle Cake, 187

Double Chocolate Pound Cake, 183
Doughnut Cake, 190
Lemon Raspberry Cheesecake, 192
Star Cake, 195
Stars and Baseballs Cake, 218
Store-Bought Chocolate Cake, 202
Vanilla White Cake, 196
Vegan Creamcake, 194
Wonder Cake, 197
Yellow Cake, 195

Calcium, 56, 68

Cancer, 78

Candy Bar Chocolate Frosting, 205

Canola oil, 50

Caramel, 161

Carameled Apple Cake, 188–89

Carrots
Carrot Cake, 186
Curried Rice, 142
Rainbow Happy Healthy Juice, 23

Casein, 57

Casseroles
Hot Dog, Bean, and Tortilla Casserole, 134
Inside Out Manicotti Pasta Bake, 106
Layered Vegetarian Enchiladas, 129
Risotto Parmesan Butternut Squash Bake, 104
Salmon Rice Pie, 128
Spinach and Cheese Bake, 123
Upside-Down Shepherd's Pie, 126
Vegetarian Tamale Casserole, 122
Wild Rice Bake, 127

Cause You're Special, 14

Ceci. See Chickpeas

Cecilia's Gluten-Free Grocery, 144

Celiac disease, 48, 145, 146

Celiac Disease Foundation, 29

Cheese
Cheesy Little Corn Cakes, 150
Cheesy Rice Balls, 75
Cheesy Yum Dip, 34
dairy-free, 14, 15
Mommy's Mock Goldfish Crackers, 44
as source of calcium, 68
Spinach and Cheese Bake, 123

Cheesecake
Lemon Raspberry Cheesecake, 192
Vegan Creamcake, 194

Cherries
about, 84

Jumbo Vanilla Cherry Muffins, 84
Chewy Granola Bars, 42
Chicken
  Chicken Noodle Soup, 119
  Chicken Nuggets with Sweet
    Dipping Sauce, 132–33
  Hot Dog, Bean, and Tortilla
    Casserole, 134
  Tortilla Soup, 117
  Upside-Down Shepherd's Pie, 126
  Wild Rice Bake, 127
Chickpeas
  about, 32
  Bean Dip, 32
  Bean Salad, 47
Children
  cooking with, 191
  dietary guidelines for, 58
Chili-Mac, 124
Chocolate
  Candy Bar Chocolate Frosting,
    205
  Chocolate Cake, 184–85
  Chocolate Custard, 200
  Chocolate Kiss Cookies, 164
  Chocolate Rice Pudding, 172
  Cocoa Pear Tart, 191
  Double Chocolate Pound Cake,
    183
  Fancy Fruit, 211
  Flourless Gourmet Brownies, 214
  Frosted Brownies, 179
  Hershey's Milk-Free Dark Bark, 210
  Ice Cream Bowls, 212
  Jumbo Vanilla Cherry Muffins, 84
  Lemon Raspberry Topping, 193
  Mini Zebra Bites, 176
  Mini-Chip Meringues, 156
  Oh Whee Ohs, 180–81
  Pecan Candy Bars, 171
  pies, 198
  Shortbread, 165
  Store-Bought Chocolate Cake, 202
  Vanilla Chip Cookies, 154–55
  Vegan Chip Cookies, 175
  Who Wants a Twix-y Bar, 161
  Yummy Crunchies, 157
Cinnamon
  Cinnamon Applesauce, 22
  Cinnamon Crunch Snack Mix, 39
  Cinnamon Sweet Frosting, 206
Clay Dough, 219
Cocoa Pear Tart, 191
Coconut

Coconut Wheels, 162
Fuzzy Fruit Ambrosia, 36
pies, 198
On the Trail Mix, 38
Vegan Tropical Muffins, 85
Yummy Crunchies, 157
Cookies and bars
  Chocolate Kiss Cookies, 164
  Coconut Wheels, 162
  Crinkle Crunchies, 168
  Easy Multipurpose Sugar Cookie
    Dough, 163
  Flourless Gourmet Brownies, 214
  Frosted Brownies, 179
  Fruit Bars, 160
  Fun Cut-Outs, 166
  Gingerbread, 166
  Just Like Nilla Wafers, 158
  Lemon Berry Bars, 170
  Little Fingers, 177
  Marshmallow Crunchy Bar
    Cut-Outs, 182
  Mini Zebra Bites, 176
  Mini-Chip Meringues, 156
  My Madelines, 178
  Oatmeal Raisin, 174
  Oh Whee Ohs, 180–81
  origins of, 179
  Pecan Candy Bars, 171
  Shortbread, 165
  Sugar, 167
  Sugar Cookie Dough, 169
  Tea Cakes, 167
  Vanilla Chip Cookies, 154–55
  Vegan Chip Cookies, 175
  Who Wants a Twix-y Bar, 161
  Yummy Crunchies, 157
Corn
  about, 54
  Cheesy Little Corn Cakes, 150
  Corn Bread with Everything, 145
  Corn Dogs, 135
  Polenta Snack Cakes, 76
Corn syrup, 17
Cornstarch, 17
Courgette
  Layered Vegetarian Enchiladas, 129
  Polenta Snack Cakes, 76
  Courgette Sticks, 74
Crackers, Mommy's Mock
  Goldfish, 44
Cranberries
  Sweet Potato Cranberry Muffins, 81

Cream Cheese Push-in Crust, 204
Cream of tartar, 169
Cream Puffs, 213
Creamsicle Cake, 187
Creamsicle Frosting, 206
Creamy Potato Salad, 49
Crepes
  Blue Pancake Crepes with Blue
    Applesauce and Honey Syrup, 91
  Sizzling All-Purpose Tortilla
    Crepes, The, 98
Crinkle Crunchies, 168
Croutons, Cut Out, 41
Crudités, 66
Crunchy Granola Bars, 37
Cucumber Yogurt Dip, 35
Cupcakes. See Cakes
Curried Rice, 142
Custard
  Blueberry Custard, 201
  Chocolate Custard, 200
Cut Out Croutons, 41
—D—
Dairy products, recommended
  brands of, 14–15
Dairy-free cheese, 14, 15
Dairy-Free Frosting, 207
Dangerous Grains (Braly), 37
Dates, 175
De Boles, 14
Dermatitis, 77
Desserts See also Cakes; Cookies
  and bars; Frostings; Puddings
  Blueberry Custard, 201
  Brown Sugar Dough, 159
  Chocolate Custard, 200
  Cocoa Pear Tart, 191
  Cream Cheese Push-in Crust, 204
  Cream Puffs, 213
  Fancy Fruit, 211
  Frozen Yogurt Sandwiches, 26–27
  Hershey's Milk-Free Dark Bark,
    210
  Homemade Marshmallows, 209
  Ice Cream Bowls, 212
  Low-Sugar Blintzes, 215
  My Size Pies, 198–99
  Perfect Pie Crust, The, 203
Devilish Eggs, 45
Dietary guidelines, for children, 58
Dips
  Bean Dip, 32
  Cheesy Yum Dip, 34
  Cucumber Yogurt Dip, 35

Guacamole Salsa, 66
Hale and Hearty Fruit Dip, 30
Mexican Five-Layer Dip, 33
Spinach Dip, 31
Double Chocolate Pound Cake, 183
Doughnut Cake, 190
Dressings
  Honey Mustard, 138
  Ranch Dressing, 137
  Salsa Vinaigrette, 138
Drinks. See Beverages
—E—
Easy Multipurpose Sugar Cookie
  Dough, 163
Eating out, 101
Eczema, 77
Egg replacements, 17, 187
Eggs
  about, 187
  Breakfast Skillet, 95
  Devilish Eggs, 45
  Mini Quiches, 71
  Scrambled Egg Enchiladas, 97
Ener-G Chocolate Chips, 17
Ener-G Egg Replacer, 17, 187
Ener-G Foods, 14, 16, 17
EnviroKids, 16
—F—
Fancy Fruit, 211
Fettuccine Alfredo, 99
Fiber, 21, 32
Fiesta Party Pleasers, 219
Fish
  Fishy Sticks, 131
  Noodle Doodle Salad, 58
  Salmon Rice Pie, 128
  Tuna-Fish Salad, 56
Flexible Play Dough, 219
Flourless Gourmet Brownies, 214
Flours, recommended brands of,
  16–17
Food
  buying online, 14
  shopping for, 13–17
  Food Allergy and Anaphylaxis
    Network (FAAN), 114, 149
Food for Life, 14
Food intolerances/allergies
  avoiding, 132
  challenges of, 9–11
  dealing with, 137
  dermatitis and, 77
  development of, 96, 121

kissing and, 73
outgrowing, 117
peanut, 15, 38, 135
statistics on, 11, 61, 131
stress and, 106
Food preparation, 44
French Toast Bake, 94
Fried Rice, 151
From-Scratch Mac-n-Cheese, 108
Frosted Brownies, 179
Frostings
Candy Bar Chocolate Frosting, 205
Cinnamon Sweet Frosting, 206
Creamsicle Frosting, 206
Dairy-Free Frosting, 207
Honey Cream Frosting, 208
Marshmallow Frosting, 208
Royal Icing, 207
Frozen Fruit and Yogurt, 25
Frozen Yogurt Sandwiches, 26–27
Fruit *See also specific fruits*
Fancy Fruit, 211
Frozen Fruit and Yogurt, 25
Fruit and Marshmallow Sauce, 28
Fruit Bars, 160
Fruit Pies, 198
Fuzzy Fruit Ambrosia, 36
Hale and Hearty Fruit Dip, 30
Whipped Fruit Butter, 29
Fun Cut-Outs, 166
Fuzzy Fruit Ambrosia, 36
—G—
Garbanzo beans. See Chickpeas
Garlic, 47
Ginger, 52, 130
Gingerbread Cookies, 166
Glutano, 14
Gluten
sources of, 87
weight gain and, 37
Gluten Free Mall, 144
Gluten Intolerance Group of North America, 30
Gluten intolerance, information about, 59
Gluten sensitivity tests, 26
Gluten Solutions, 144
Gluten-free products, 14–17, 144
Go Cucumbers!, 48
Goat yogurt, 24–25
Good Morning Enchilada Strata, 96
Grandma's Tamale Casserole, 121
Granola

Chewy Granola Bars, 42
Crunchy Granola Bars, 37
Green Bean Bake, 148
Green Chili Bean Bake, 149
Grits, 76
Grocery stores, requesting items from, 13
Guacamole Salsa, 66
—H—
Hagaman, Bette, 110
Hale and Hearty Fruit Dip, 30
Ham
Fried Rice, 151
Hot and Yummy Pockets, 70
Mock Top Ramen Soup, 120
Scrambled Egg Enchiladas, 97
Wild Rice Bake, 127
Happy Burgers, 139
Harvest Soup, 118
Heart disease, apples and, 20
Hershey's, 210
Hershey's Milk-Free Dark Bark, 210
Hidden Food Allergies (Astor), 90
Homemade Marshmallows, 209
Homemade Pizza Dough, 110
Honey, 39, 43
Honey Cream Frosting, 208
Honey Mustard, 138
Honey Mustard Snack Mix, 40
Honey Syrup, 92
Horchata Rice Drink, 24
Hot and Yummy Pockets, 70
Hot dogs
Corn Dogs, 135
Hot Dog, Bean, and Tortilla Casserole, 134
—I—
Ice Cream Bowls, 212
Icings. *See* Frostings
Imagine Foods, 15
Ingredients
buying online, 14
calling customer service line about, 40
identifying, on labels, 114, 138
shopping for, 13–17
Inside Out Manicotti Pasta Bake, 106
—J—
Jell-O pudding, 15
Jicama, 31
Juice, Rainbow Happy Healthy, 23
Jumbo Vanilla Cherry Muffins, 84
Just Like Nilla Wafers, 158

—K—
Kidney beans. See Beans
Kids' Pizza-Pizza, 109
Knorr, 17
Kraft products, 15
—L—
Lactaid, 14
Lactose intolerance, 24, 49, 126
Lamb
Pastitsio, 102–3
Layered Vegetarian Enchiladas, 129
Lecithin, 108
Lemon
Lemon Berry Bars, 170
Lemon Poppy Seed Muffins, 79
Lemon Raspberry Cheesecake, 192
Lemon Raspberry Topping, 193
Little Fingers, 177
Little Slugger's Party, 218
Log Cabin syrups, 17
Low/No Sugar Baked Rice Pudding, 173
Low-Sugar Blintzes, 215
Lundberg Farms, 16
Lundberg Rice, 14
—M—
Macaroni
From-Scratch Mac-n-Cheese, 108
Macaroni and Easy Cheese, 107
Macaroni Salad, 55
Magnesium, 56
Maple syrup, 86
Marshmallow
Fruit and Marshmallow Sauce, 28
Homemade Marshmallows, 209
Marshmallow Crunchy Bar Cut-Outs, 182
Marshmallow Frosting, 208
McDonald's, 139
Mexican dishes
Good Morning Enchilada Strata, 96
Grandma's Tamale Casserole, 121
Green Chili Bean Bake, 149
Hot Dog, Bean, and Tortilla Casserole, 134
Layered Vegetarian Enchiladas, 129
Mexican Five-Layer Dip, 33
Mexican Pizza, 68
Mexican-Style Baked Beans, 146
Nacho Quesadillas, 69
Scrambled Egg Enchiladas, 97
Taco Salad Meal, 136

Tortilla Soup, 117
Vegetarian Tamale Casserole, 122
Milk allergies, 49, 57, 148
Mini Quiches, 71
Mini Scones with Maple Drizzles, 86
Mini Zebra Bites, 176
Mini-Chip Meringues, 156
Mock Top Ramen Soup, 120
Mommy's Mock Goldfish Crackers, 44
Morning Bars, 43
Mrs. Butterworth's syrups, 17
Muffins
Awesome Blueberries, 78
Banana Bread, 77
Bran and Raisin, 82
Jumbo Vanilla Cherry, 84
Lemon Poppy Seed, 79
PB and Banana Chip, 80
Sweet Potato Cranberry, 81
Vegan Tropical, 85
Very Berry, 83
Mushrooms, Pizza Stuffed, 115
My Madelines, 178
My Size Pies, 198–99
—N—
Nacho Quesadillas, 69
Navy beans. *See* Beans
Nestlé's Tollhouse Chocolate Chips, 17
Noodles
See also Pasta dishes
Broccoli Beef Noodles, 130
Chicken Noodle Soup, 119
Mock Top Ramen Soup, 120
Noodle Doodle Salad, 58
Pizza Noodles, 116
Potato Noodles with Sour Cream Alfredo and Chives, 100
Nut allergies, 15, 38, 135
—O—
Oats
Chewy Granola Bars, 42
Crunchy Granola Bars, 37
gluten and, 87
Morning Bars, 43
Oatmeal Raisin, 174
Oh Whee Ohs, 180–81
Oils, 113, 152
Olive oil, 152
On the Trail Mix, 38
Oranges
Fuzzy Fruit Ambrosia, 36

Rainbow Happy Healthy Juice, 23
—P—
Pacific Rice, 15
Pamela's, 16
Pancakes
  Blue Pancake Crepes with Blue
    Applesauce and Honey Syrup, 91
  Buttermilk Pancakes, 90
  Pancake Torte, 93
Parmesan, 104
Party ideas, 218–19
pasta
  recommended brands, 14
Pasta dishes
  See also Macaroni; Noodles
  Alfredo and Chives, 101
  Chili-Mac, 124
  Fettuccine Alfredo, 99
  Inside Out Manicotti Pasta Bake,
    106
  Pastitsio, 102–3
  Very Best Spaghetti, The, 105
Pastitsio, 102–3
PB & J Roll-Ups, 73
PB and Banana Chip Muffins, 80
Peanut allergies, 15, 38, 135
Peanut Allergy Answer Book
  (Young), 15
Peanut oil, 113
Pears
  Cocoa Pear Tart, 191
  Rainbow Happy Healthy Juice, 23
Pecans
  Pecan Sweets, 171
  Tea Cakes, 167
Pepperoni
  Hot and Yummy Pockets, 70
  Pizza Noodles, 116
  Pizza Stuffed Mushrooms, 115
  Upside-Down Pizza, 113
Peppers, 51
Perfect Pie Crust, The, 203
Philadelphia cream cheese, 14
Phytochemicals, 23, 78
Pies
  Banana, 198
  Butterscotch, 198
  Chocolate, 198
  Coconut, 198
  Cream Cheese Push-in Crust, 204
  Fruit, 198
  My Size Pies, 198–99
  Perfect Pie Crust, The, 203

Salmon Rice Pie, 128
  Upside-Down Shepherd's Pie, 126
Pineapple
  Fuzzy Fruit Ambrosia, 36
  Vegan Tropical Muffins, 85
Pink Applesauce, 21
Pinquito beans. See Beans
Pinto beans. See Beans
Pizza
  Homemade Pizza Dough, 110
  Kids' Pizza-Pizza, 109
  Mexican Pizza, 68
  Pizza Bites, 67
  Pizza Noodles, 116
  Pizza Stuffed Mushrooms, 115
  Polenta Crust Pizza, 114
  Red Sauce, 111
  Rice Cracker Personal Pizzas, 46
  Upside-Down Pizza, 113
  Vegetarian Potato Pizza, 112
  White Sauce, 111
Play Dough, Flexible, 219
Plums, 60
Polenta
  about, 76
  Polenta Crust Pizza, 114
  Polenta Snack Cakes, 76
Pork
  See also Ham
  Pizza Noodles, 116
  Scrambled Egg Enchiladas, 97
  Upside-Down Pizza, 113
potato starch, 17
Potatoes
  about, 72
  Baked Potato Nachos, 65
  Creamy Potato Salad, 49
  Kids' Pizza-Pizza, 109
  Potato Noodles with Sour Cream
    Alfredo and Chives, 100
  Puffy Potatoes, 72
  Red Potatoes, 147
  Sloppy Joe Potato Skillet, 125
  Two Potato Salad, 50
  Upside-Down Shepherd's Pie, 126
  Vegetarian Potato Pizza, 112
Poultry. See Chicken; Turkey
Pretzels, 40
Princess Dream Party, 218
Puddings
  Apple Rice Pudding, 172
  Chocolate Rice, 172
  Low/No Sugar Baked Rice

Pudding, 173
  Plain, 172
  Raisin, 172
Puffy Potatoes, 72
Pumpkin
  Mini Scones with Maple Drizzles,
    86
—Q—
Quiches, Mini, 71
—R—
Rainbow Happy Healthy Juice, 23
Raisins, 173
  about, 82
  Bran and Raisin Muffins, 82
  Oatmeal Raisin, 174
  Raising Pudding, 172
Ranch Dressing, 137
Raspberries
  Lemon Berry Bars, 170
  Lemon Raspberry Cheesecake,
    192
  Lemon Raspberry Topping, 193
  phytochemicals in, 78
  Pink Applesauce, 21
  varieties of, 193
  Very Berry Muffins, 83
Real Foods, 16
Red pepper
  Layered Vegetarian Enchiladas,
    129
Red Potatoes, 147
Red Sauce, 111
Restaurant meals, 101
Rice
  Apple Rice Pudding, 172
  Brown Rice and Apple Salad, 53
  Cheesy Rice Balls, 75
  Curried Rice, 142
  Fried Rice, 151
  Horchata Rice Drink, 24
  Low/No Sugar Baked Rice
    Pudding, 173
  Rice Pinwheels, 62–63
  Rice Snowballs, 61
  Risotto Parmesan Butternut
    Squash Bake, 104
  Salmon Rice Pie, 128
  Salsa Bean and Rice Salad, 54
  Thai Rolls, 59
  Turkey Rice Salad, 51
  Ubu, 64
  Wild Rice Bake, 127
Rice Cracker Personal Pizzas, 46
Rice flour, 13, 16

Rice starch, 17
Rice Vinegar Asian Salad, 52
Risotto Parmesan Butternut
  Squash Bake, 104
Royal Icing, 207
—S—
Salad dressings
  Honey Mustard, 138
  Ranch Dressing, 137
  Salsa Vinaigrette, 138
Salads
  Bean Salad, 47
  Brown Rice and Apple Salad, 53
  Creamy Potato Salad, 49
  Go Cucumbers!, 48
  Macaroni Salad, 55
  Noodle Doodle Salad, 58
  Rice Vinegar Asian Salad, 52
  Salsa Bean and Rice Salad, 54
  Taco Salad Meal, 136
  Tuna-Fish Salad, 56
  Turkey Rice Salad, 51
  Two Potato Salad, 50
  Vegan Salad, 57
Salmon Rice Pie, 128
Salsa Bean and Rice Salad, 54
Salsa Vinaigrette, 138
Sauces
  Caramel, 188–89
  Fruit and Marshmallow Sauce, 28
  Lemon Raspberry Topping, 193
  Red Sauce, 111
  Sweet Dipping Sauce, 133
  Tartar Sauce, 131
  White Sauce, 111
Scones with Maple Drizzles,
  Mini, 86
Scrambled Egg Enchiladas, 97
seasonings, 17
Shortbread, 165
Shrimp
  Mock Top Ramen Soup, 120
Side dishes
  Cheesy Little Corn Cakes, 150
  Corn Bread with Everything, 145
  Curried Rice, 142
  Fried Rice, 151
  Green Bean Bake, 148
  Green Chili Bean Bake, 149
  Mexican-Style Baked Beans, 146
  Red Potatoes, 147
  Sweet Potato Hash, 152
  Teriyaki Veggie Spears, 143

Whipped Sweet Potatoes, 144

Sizzling All-Purpose Tortilla Crepes, The, 98

Sloppy Joe Potato Skillet, 125

Snacks

See also Beverages; Dips; Salads

applesauces, 20–22

Baked Potato Nachos, 65

Cheesy Rice Balls, 75

Chewy Granola Bars, 42

Cinnamon Crunch Snack Mix, 39

Crunchy Granola Bars, 37

Cut Out Croutons, 41

Devilish Eggs, 45

Frozen Fruit and Yogurt, 25

Frozen Yogurt Sandwiches, 26–27

Fuzzy Fruit Ambrosia, 36

Honey Mustard Snack Mix, 40

Hot and Yummy Pockets, 70

Mexican Pizza, 68

Mini Quiches, 71

Mommy's Mock Goldfish Crackers, 44

Morning Bars, 43

Nacho Quesadillas, 69

PB & J Roll-Ups, 73

Pizza Bites, 67

Polenta Snack Cakes, 76

Puffy Potatoes, 72

recommended brands of, 15–16

Rice Cracker Personal Pizzas, 46

Rice Pinwheels, 62–63

Rice Snowballs, 61

Spring Rolls, 60

Thai Rolls, 59

On the Trail Mix, 38

Ubu, 64

Courgette Sticks, 74

Soluble fiber, 21

Soups

Chicken Noodle Soup, 119

Harvest Soup, 118

Mock Top Ramen Soup, 120

Tortilla Soup, 117

Soy sauce, 17

Soybeans, 147

Spectrum, 17, 168

Spinach

Salmon Rice Pie, 128

Spinach and Cheese Bake, 123

Spinach Dip, 31

Spring Rolls, 60

Squash, 74

Harvest Soup, 118

Risotto Parmesan Butternut Squash Bake, 104

Star Cake, 195

Stars and Baseballs Cake, 218

Store-Bought Chocolate Cake, 202

Strawberries

Applesauce Parfait, 22

Fancy Fruit, 211

Fuzzy Fruit Ambrosia, 36

phytochemicals in, 78

Pink Applesauce, 21

Very Berry Muffins, 83

Stress, 106

Sugar, 17, 154

Sugar Cookie Dough, 169

Sugar Cookie Dough, Easy Multipurpose, 163

Sugar substitutes, 157

supermarket, requesting items from, 13

Sushi

Rice Pinwheels, 62–63

Sweet Dipping Sauce, 133

Sweet potatoes

Sweet Potato Cranberry Muffins, 81

Sweet Potato Hash, 152

Whipped Sweet Potatoes, 144

Syrups

Honey Syrup, 92

recommended brands, 17

—T—

Taco Salad Meal, 136

Tamari soy sauce, 17

tapioca starch, 17

Tart, Cocoa Pear, 191

Tartar Sauce, 131

Tea Cakes, 167

Teriyaki Veggie Spears, 143

Thai Rolls, 59

Tillamook, 15

Tinkyada, 14

Tortilla Soup, 117

Tuna

Noodle Doodle Salad, 58

Tuna-Fish Salad, 56

Turkey

Grandma's Tamale Casserole, 121

Happy Burgers, 139

Pizza Noodles, 116

Sloppy Joe Potato Skillet, 125

Turkey Rice Salad, 51

Upside-Down Pizza, 113

Upside-Down Shepherd's Pie, 126

Wild Rice Bake, 127

Two Potato Salad, 50

—U—

Ubu, 64

Uncle Ben's Cream of Rice cereal, 16

Upside-Down Pizza, 113

Upside-Down Shepherd's Pie, 126

—V—

Vanilla Chip Cookies, 154–55

Vanilla extract, 17, 163

Vanilla White Cake, 196

Vans, 16

Vegan Chip Cookies, 175

Vegan Creamcake, 194

Vegan Salad, 57

Vegan Tropical Muffins, 85

Vegans, 104

Vegetables

See also specific vegetables

Teriyaki Veggie Spears, 143

Vegetarian Potato Pizza, 112

Vegetarian Tamale Casserole, 122

Vegetarians, 104

Vermont Nut Free Chocolates, 16

Very Berry Muffins, 83

Very Best Spaghetti, The, 105

Vitamin C, 51

—W—

Water-soluble fiber, 21, 32

Weight gain, gluten and gluten and, 37

Wheat allergens, 10, 53, 62

Whey Low, 17

Whipped Fruit Butter, 29

Whipped Sweet Potatoes, 144

White Sauce, 111

Who Wants a Twix-y Bar, 161

Wild Rice Bake, 127

Wonder Cake, 197

Wood, Robert A., 96

—Y—

Yellow Cake, 195

Yogurt

Cucumber Yogurt Dip, 35

Frozen Fruit and Yogurt, 25

Frozen Yogurt Sandwiches, 26–27

goat, 24–25

Young, Michael, 15

Yummy Crunchies, 157